Happy Anniversary
#19
2-19-91

KANSAS

"Kansas' Enterprises" by Judith Galas

Produced in cooperation with the Kansas Department of Commerce

Windsor Publications, Inc.
Chatsworth, California

KANSAS

America, Center Stage

A Contemporary Portrait by Linda Swander McMullen and Ron Welch

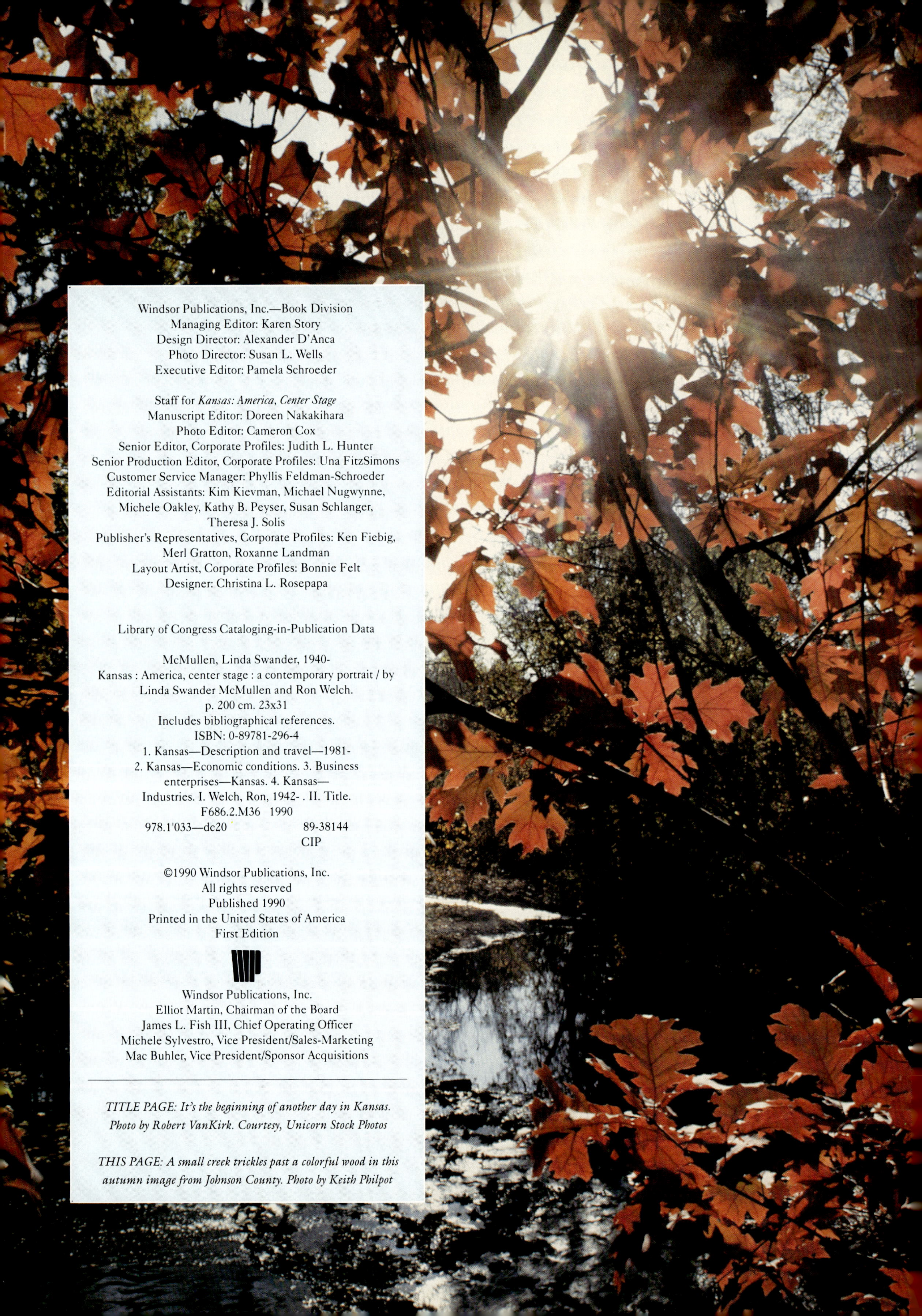

Windsor Publications, Inc.—Book Division
Managing Editor: Karen Story
Design Director: Alexander D'Anca
Photo Director: Susan L. Wells
Executive Editor: Pamela Schroeder

Staff for *Kansas: America, Center Stage*
Manuscript Editor: Doreen Nakakihara
Photo Editor: Cameron Cox
Senior Editor, Corporate Profiles: Judith L. Hunter
Senior Production Editor, Corporate Profiles: Una FitzSimons
Customer Service Manager: Phyllis Feldman-Schroeder
Editorial Assistants: Kim Kievman, Michael Nugwynne, Michele Oakley, Kathy B. Peyser, Susan Schlanger, Theresa J. Solis
Publisher's Representatives, Corporate Profiles: Ken Fiebig, Merl Gratton, Roxanne Landman
Layout Artist, Corporate Profiles: Bonnie Felt
Designer: Christina L. Rosepapa

Library of Congress Cataloging-in-Publication Data

McMullen, Linda Swander, 1940-
Kansas : America, center stage : a contemporary portrait / by Linda Swander McMullen and Ron Welch.
p. 200 cm. 23x31
Includes bibliographical references.
ISBN: 0-89781-296-4
1. Kansas—Description and travel—1981- 2. Kansas—Economic conditions. 3. Business enterprises—Kansas. 4. Kansas—Industries. I. Welch, Ron, 1942- . II. Title.
F686.2.M36 1990
978.1'033—dc20 89-38144
CIP

Published 1990
Printed in the United States of America
First Edition

Windsor Publications, Inc.
Elliot Martin, Chairman of the Board
James L. Fish III, Chief Operating Officer
Michele Sylvestro, Vice President/Sales-Marketing
Mac Buhler, Vice President/Sponsor Acquisitions

TITLE PAGE: It's the beginning of another day in Kansas. Photo by Robert VanKirk. Courtesy, Unicorn Stock Photos

THIS PAGE: A small creek trickles past a colorful wood in this autumn image from Johnson County. Photo by Keith Philpot

CONTENTS

PART II
KANSAS MEANS BUSINESS 67

PART III
KANSAS' ENTERPRISES 121

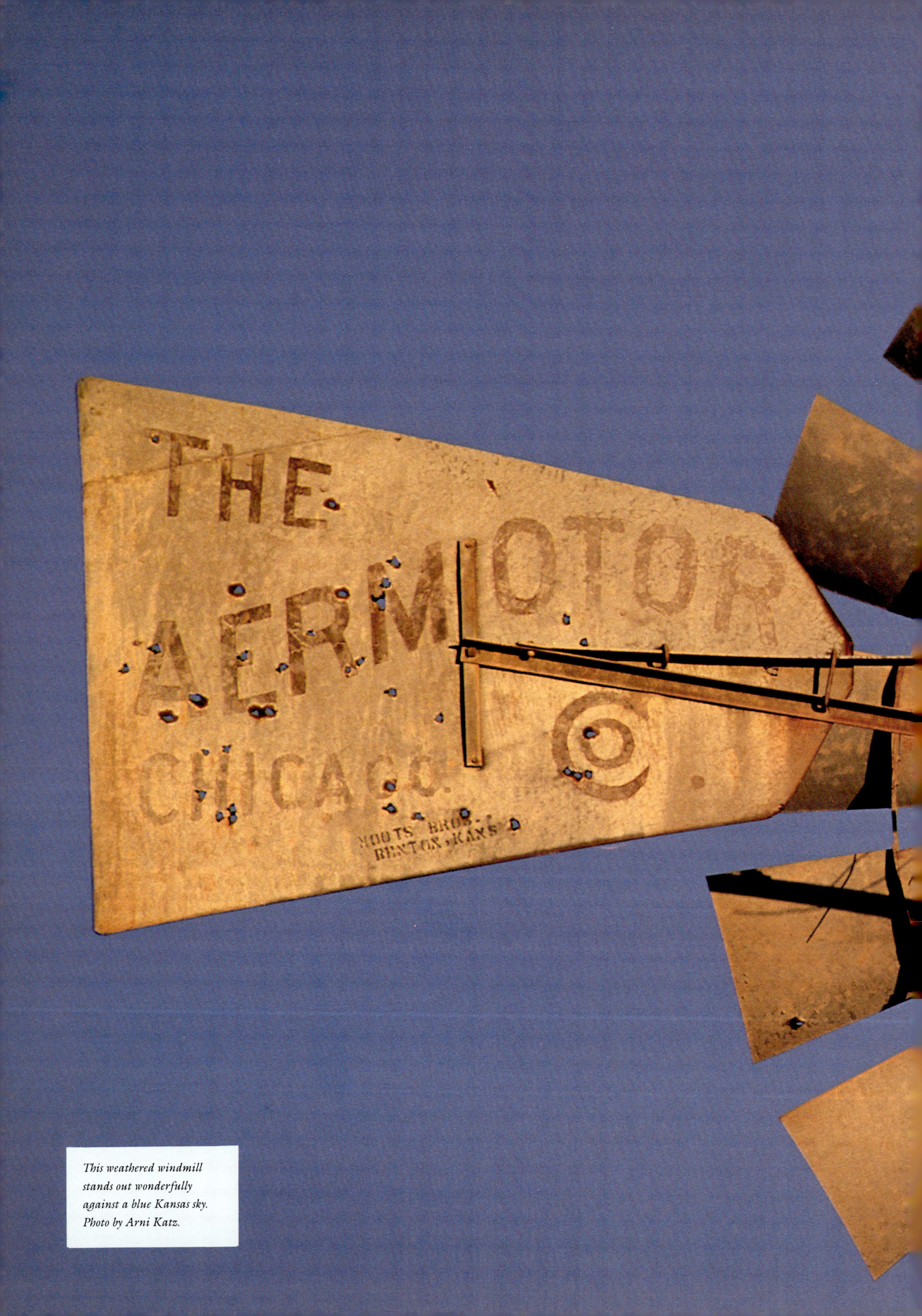

This weathered windmill stands out wonderfully against a blue Kansas sky. Photo by Arni Katz.

Kansas truly is America, center stage. Geographically, it is the focal point of the 48 contiguous states. Agriculturally, it is a cornucopia for the world's tables. Philosophically, it is a place where people retain the values and patriotism that have made our nation great.

This book is not a history of Kansas, nor of Kansans, although it will delve briefly into the pasts of both. Rather, it is an affirmation of what is currently taking place to ensure that the state continues to prosper into the twenty-first century.

What is Kansas?

Physically, it is a 208-by-411-mile state shaped like a rectangle. The Missouri River cuts a small, irregular edge through its upper right-hand corner.

Kansas is bounded by Missouri to the east, Nebraska to the north, Colorado to the west, and Oklahoma to the south.

Topographically, the state is hilly, though several vast expanses of plains are located in the central and western regions. The earth is fertile and contains abundant natural resources. Kansas is America's leading producer of helium and also has major reserves of natural gas, petroleum, gypsum, and salt.

Climatically, the state has four distinct seasons. The average annual temperature is 55 degrees.

The majority of Kansans—more than 70 percent of the population—lives in an urban setting. The eastern half of the state is the most populous. Western Kansas is predominantly rural.

Kansans have traditionally been an ingenious lot. When faced with a challenging problem, they have responded with a number of inventions that have benefited mankind. For example, two residents of Morrowville, Jim Cummings and J. Earl McLeod, patented the world's first bulldozer in 1925. Cummings had observed the laborious back-filling, by mules and slip scrapers, of an oil pipeline trench being built from Wyoming to Missouri. He knew there had to be a better way of doing it. After explaining his idea to Sinclair Oil Company officials, he was encouraged to build his bulldozer. They gave him three days to come up with a finished product. McLeod drafted a design in four hours and the rest, as has often been said, is history.

Dr. Samuel J. Crumbine, of the Kansas State Board of Health, and schoolteacher Frank H. Rose conceived and developed the flyswatter. Crumbine had been looking for a way to exterminate flies because they were spreaders of typhoid fever. While attending a softball game in 1905, he heard some fans yell, "Swat it, swat the ball." He thought, why not "swat the fly"? Rose picked up on the idea and, with a yardstick and wire screen, produced the first flyswatter.

Kansas women also have made their mark. Topekan Georgia Neese

PROLOGUE

Gray was the first female treasurer of the United States, from 1949 to 1953. Nancy Landon Kassebaum was the first woman to be elected to the U.S. Senate without originally having been appointed to fill an unexpired term. Susanna Madora Salter was the nation's first woman mayor, serving the community of Argonia beginning in 1887. Lucy Hobbs Taylor was the first fully trained female dentist in the world. She practiced in Lawrence from 1867 to 1907. In 1897 Topekan Lutie Lytle was the first black woman admitted to the practice of law in the United States. In 1918 Nellie Cline of Larned became the first woman lawyer to appear before the U.S. Supreme Court.

Amelia Earhart, an Atchison native, was the first woman granted a pilot's license by the National Aeronautics Association. She was also the first female to fly solo across the Atlantic Ocean.

These individuals, and many others like Dwight David Eisenhower, Joe Engle, Steve Hawley, and Ron Evans, personify what was described in an early twentieth-century essay as "The Kansas Spirit." The spirit, it was said, "is one that finds something exhilarating in the challenge of an extreme difficulty."

Eisenhower overcame numerous obstacles to become president of the United States. Engle, Hawley, and Evans, three Kansas astronauts, were instrumental in expanding man's knowledge of space.

To understand what drove these Kansans to excel and continues to propel others toward new heights in business, education, politics, and additional fields of endeavor, one must look at Kansas' history—a history fraught with an adversity that prompted its forefathers to adopt the Latin motto *Ad Astra per Aspera* (To the stars through difficulties) after statehood was realized in 1861.

The earliest known inhabitants of Kansas were a nomadic people, named the Paleo Indians by archaeologists. These hunter-gatherers lived here some 12,000 years ago. The first European contact with the Paleo Indians took place in 1540-41, when the Spanish conquistador Francisco Vasquez de Coronado met Plains Apaches near present-day Fort Dodge. Coronado's travels also took him to central Kansas, where he encountered the agriculturally oriented Wichitas. Both tribes, and others living in the area, were destined to be displaced from their hunting grounds and farmlands some 300 years later, by white settlers arriving on trails with names such as Oregon and Santa Fe.

The new Kansas immigrants built forts and towns and fenced in the prairie. In 1854 Kansas was organized as a territory under the Kansas-Nebraska Act. The legislation removed the final barrier to legally extending slavery into the West. Whether either territory became a "slave state" was to be determined by its inhabitants. Proponents of the act generally thought that people opposed to slavery would settle in Nebraska and those favoring it would make Kansas their home.

Such was not the case. Violent conflicts were waged over the slavery question in Kansas and the territory became known worldwide as "Bleeding Kansas." Eventually the free-state advocates won out in both territories. Neither permitted slavery.

When the Civil War was resolved and slavery was abolished throughout the land, the nation looked west again and settlers came streaming into Kansas. Two major factors that contributed to permanent settlement were the introduction of Turkey Red wheat, by Mennonites from Russia in 1874, and the building of railroads in the state.

Turkey Red is a hardy winter wheat that is ideally suited to Kansas crop-growing conditions. Bountiful harvests of the grain enabled the state to become the number one producer of wheat in the nation.

The railroads' arrival benefited virtually all Kansans, but particularly cattle shippers. Cow towns like Abilene, Ellsworth, and Dodge City became major shipping points for animals bound for packing plants in Chicago and the east. Topeka, Newton, Wichita, Dodge City, and other communities grew and prospered as rail repair and supply depots for companies including the Union Pacific and the Atchison, Topeka & Santa Fe.

Although agriculture continued to be the mainstay of the state's economy into the twentieth century, manufacturing made inroads. Several carmakers tried to turn Kansas into a Detroit of the West. The Great Smith automobile, built in Topeka, enjoyed limited success. It was the first car to be driven to the top of Colorado's Pikes Peak.

In 1925 Walter H. Beech, a salesman and test pilot for the Swallow Airplane Company of Wichita, organized the Travel Air Company, the forerunner of Beech Aircraft Co. It was a move destined to have a dramatic impact on the Kansas economy that continues to this day. By 1929 the company was producing more than 25 percent of all the airplanes manufactured in America. Kansas was on its way to establishing itself as the U.S. leader in general aviation aircraft production. Wichita is still known as the "Air Capital City."

Clyde V. Cessna, who according to a newspaper article "began to fly when airships were made out of fishing poles," was named Travel Air's first president. Like Beech, he hankered to build his own "crate." In 1927 he started the Cessna Aircraft Company, also in Wichita.

Another famous aviation name, Boeing, established its presence in Wichita in 1927. The company played a giant role in America's war efforts in the 1940s, producing bombers like the B-29 Superfortress. In the 1950s its assembly lines turned out B-47 and B-52 bombers. Now Boeing Military Airplanes is a center for aircraft engineering, fabrication, and assembly. It does extensive avionics development for U.S. Air Force bomber and tanker fleets and civilian jetliners.

The last major aircraft company to

locate in Kansas was Learjet in the 1960s.

Just as the state's civilian aircraft companies, and many other Kansas businesses, have made significant contributions to our national defense, so have three important Kansas military bases. They also are major employers in the communities where they are located.

Fort Leavenworth is the oldest continuously garrisoned military post west of the Mississippi River, having been established in 1827. The U.S. Army Command and General Staff College has operated at Fort Leavenworth since 1881. More than 54,000 United States and Allied officers, including George S. Patton, Douglas MacArthur, Dwight David Eisenhower, and Omar Bradley, have attended the army's senior tactical school.

Fort Riley, near Junction City, is the headquarters of the "Big Red One" First Infantry Division. The post also was the home of the U.S. Cavalry, and famous officers like J.E.B. Stuart and George Armstrong Custer served there.

McConnell AFB, in Wichita, has had many different roles since its founding. It was an F-105 fighter-bomber training base during the Vietnam War and later was headquarters for a missile wing. Its newest tenants are B-1B bombers and support units.

Following World War II, Kansas settled into a regular routine of agricultural and industrial production. Most citizens were content with the quality of life they enjoyed in the state. Some that weren't, however, started on a course that was to change the face of America.

Thirteen black parents tried to enroll their children in an all-white elementary school in Topeka in 1950. At the time, 17 states and the District of Columbia had laws on their books requiring racial segregation in public schools. The unanimous U.S. Supreme Court verdict won by the parents, in litigation known as *Brown v. Board of Education of Topeka,* declared, "Separate educational facilities are inherently unequal." The gauntlet had been thrown in Kansas. Blacks had won the first round in what was to become the turbulent civil rights movement.

During the 1960s, 1970s, and 1980s the Kansas economy shifted dramatically, from dependence on agriculture to diversity. Surplus harvests and resultant low crop prices forced many families to leave their land and seek work in urban areas. Numerous small towns that relied on farmers and ranchers to patronize their businesses lost population, schools, banks, and other amenities necessary for their survival.

In contrast, cities and counties near metropolitan centers have prospered. Overland Park, Lenexa, and Olathe have grown rapidly because of their proximity to Kansas City. Johnson County, where the three are located, is now one of America's most affluent counties.

Wichita, the state's largest city, has a population of close to 300,000. Industries there attract workers from as far away as Oklahoma.

Although large manufacturing plants and corporations are significant contributors to the quality of life Kansans enjoy, small businesses have blossomed and prospered, too, some of them in specialized fields that most people wouldn't associate with the state.

Holiday Mansion in Salina, for example, makes luxury houseboats that are used in ocean ports and on the Gulf of Mexico. Kansas City's American Walnut Company produces some of the finest gun stocks in the world. Sabetha's Wenger Manufacturing Company is a leading inventor and installer of extrusion equipment.

Entrepreneurs also have found Kansas to be a good place to start a business. One "Horatio Alger" story is that of the Carney brothers, who opened their first Pizza Hut in Wichita in 1958.

Complementing Kansas' economic growth has been a change in the leisure activities of its citizens. Kansans continue to enjoy some of the finest hunting in the world, and fishing and boating on the state's many lakes are superb! Excellent museums and professional and amateur theater companies draw well. And the construction of modern civic centers and coliseums in cities such as Salina, Wichita, and Topeka has enabled many citizens to routinely attend events like ballets, performances by renowned artists, indoor auto racing, and special interest expositions heretofore not scheduled because of a lack of facilities.

The Kansas Coliseum is home to Wichita's Major Indoor Soccer League team, the "Wings." The Wichita Wranglers baseball team is the Texas League affiliate of the San Diego Padres. And for players on the Continental Basketball Association team "Topeka Sizzlers," who play at the Kansas Expocentre's Landon Arena, it's only one step up to the National Basketball Association.

Voters recently authorized changes in the Kansas constitution that permit liquor by the drink on a county-option basis, pari-mutuel wagering, and a lottery.

As the twenty-first century nears, Kansas is vibrant. Its citizens are ready to tackle the challenges of today and tomorrow that accompany continued growth. They know that they've responded well to the adversities of the past and will do so again in the future. They look forward to building a better Kansas: one that will shine bright when others look at America, center stage.

This scene is in keeping with the state song, "Home on the Range." Photo by Herbert L. Stormont. Courtesy, Unicorn Stock Photos

PART

I

THE HEART AND SPIRIT OF KANSAS

By Linda Swander McMullen

Fans from all backgrounds cheer the big rivals on at a homecoming game between the University of Kansas Jayhawks and the Kansas State University Wildcats. Photo by Arni Katz

1

THE PEOPLE

Meeting the people of Kansas today might make it hard to remember that living here was a different matter not so long ago. In his introduction to Joanna Stratton's book *Pioneer Women*, Arthur M. Schlesinger, Jr., reminds the reader that "the experience of inventing Kansas had been so desperate that only the purest faith and mightiest will could survive."

Early-day Kansans built ranches, planted corn and wheat, laid out towns, operated one-room schoolhouses, and made a wilderness habitable. They survived prairie fires, blizzards, tornadoes, grasshoppers, rattlesnakes, border wars in the 1850s, Indian raids, coyotes, wolves, droughts, and any number of calamities that would have turned back the less stouthearted.

While the first permanent white settlement was established at Fort Leavenworth in 1827, immigration did not begin in earnest until 1854. Since then Kansas has produced its fair share of famous folks, including a president of the United States, Dwight D. Eisenhower. Atchison aviatrix Amelia Earhart was a heroine, and in her own way so was temperance advocate Carry Nation, who took her hatchet to the saloons of Kansas. Track stars Glenn Cunningham and Jim Ryun made headlines when they set world records in the mile run. In 1958 two Wichita brothers named Carney started making pizzas in a building behind their father's grocery store and changed the eating habits of America. Today their creation, Pizza Hut restaurants, can be found all over the United States and in 26 foreign countries. The list goes on, and like any other state Kansas enjoys bragging about its noteworthy sons and daughters. But it is the not so famous, the everyday people, who have left the greatest legacy to the state and continue to do so today.

These people of Kansas—whether descendants of the pioneers who came in ox-drawn covered wagons and on crowded

The state capitol in Topeka, dedicated in 1903, took more than three decades to complete. Courtesy, Unicorn Stock Photos

trains or more recent arrivals attracted by career opportunities, the educational system, or the advantages synonymous with living in the state's towns and cities—personify its robust spirit. Like the immigrants who went before them, they do not back down when challenged. They possess patience, pride, friendliness, and a strong work ethic, all of which continue to keep the state at center stage.

The 1989 Labor Market Survey of Kansas lists a nonfarm wage and salary employment total of 1,060,900 persons. Nearly 25 percent of the people are employed in wholesale and retail trade. Federal, state, and local governments employ 20 percent of the work force as do service-oriented businesses. Nearly 18 percent work in manufacturing and the remainder is divided among jobs in transportation and public utilities, financial and insurance institutions, construction, and mining. Farm employment totals 57,200 persons.

Within the confines of this book it is impossible to make an extensive introduction to this population which numbers approximately 2,495,000. But perhaps by visiting with a few Kansans, some insight will be gained into the state's greatest resource—its people.

LEWIS L. McLAUGLIN

Lewis L. McLauglin "hung his shingle out" in Marysville more than half a century ago, and for most of the time since he has served the cause of justice in Kansas. He was the county attorney for Marshall County for 14 years and 21st District Judge for 24 years. Even though he's been retired since 1975, McLauglin still takes assignments from the state supreme court to fill in when there is a vacancy on the bench or to help out when the caseload is heavy. He is a past president of the

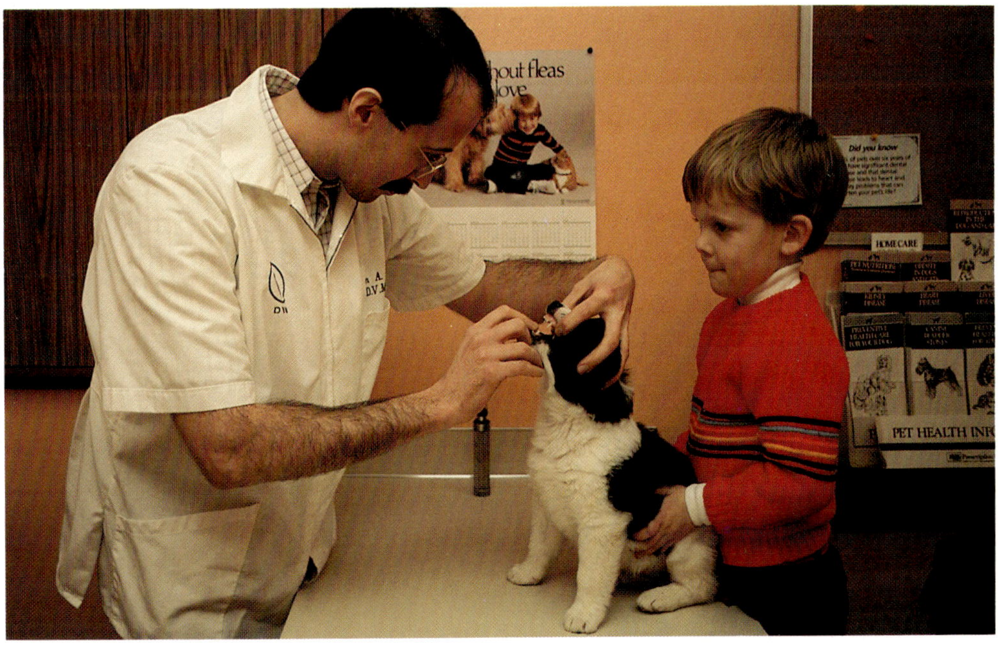

A veterinarian checks this puppy's teeth under the watchful eye of its four-year-old companion. Photo by Karen Mullen. Courtesy, Unicorn Stock Photos

Kansas County Attorneys Association and of the District Judges Association.

Upon the announcement of McLauglin's pending retirement, the *Manhattan Mercury* said of the judge in an editorial on December 5, 1974:

He was thoroughly dedicated to the highest criteria and ideals of his profession. He is a man who genuinely enjoys the personal associations that are attendant to his duties.

Any district in Kansas seeking a man of dignity, fairness, unimpeachable character and humanitarian impulses could not have done better than to have picked Lewis McLauglin for its bench.

Pretty auspicious record for a "country boy from Axtell," McLauglin will tell you. And that's where his serpentine route to the Kansas bench began.

McLauglin reminisced about the 1920s and 1930s. After high school he enrolled at nearby Highland Community College for two years and then spent some time at the University of Kansas. He left to teach school at Smith Center but only stayed there one year. That job paid $90 a month, so when he was offered a position as a physical education teacher at $140 a month in Kansas City, Missouri, he said "yes."

"Before I went to Kansas City, I decided I'd better go over to KU and learn a little more about teaching phys ed," McLauglin related. "I studied tumbling and gymnastics and Dr. James Naismith was one of my teachers." Naismith had invented the game of basketball in 1891.

It was in Kansas City that he decided on a legal career, attending night classes at the Kansas City University School of Law, now part of the University of Missouri at Kansas City. It was also in Kansas City that he met his wife of 57 years, Helen Frances Litsch, also a physical education teacher in the Kansas City, Missouri, schools.

"I didn't have a car so we did our courting in a friend's rumble seat on the way to football games in Columbia and Lawrence," McLauglin recalled. "On Friday nights we used to go down to a place on Southwest Boulevard where the boiled shrimp was free with a 25-cent beer."

Among the more rewarding of Kansas' jobs are those offered by the fire department. Photo by Jim Shippee. Courtesy, Unicorn Stock Photos

The McLauglins still enjoy a boiled shrimp gathering, and the judge considers himself the best authority around on its preparation. Like most Kansans they also enjoy a steak dinner, and their favorite place for that is Bob's Steakhouse in Seneca, a usual stop on the way home from visiting their daughter, Ellen Bradbury, and her three children, who live in Mission Hills.

As for the judicial system in the state, McLauglin says it's a lot more complicated than it used to be. The district in which he presided covered Marshall, Riley, and Clay counties. When he started practice Marshall County had a population of 25,000. Now the population is half that. He cited Johnson County as another area where the population has changed.

"They used to have two district judges, now there are 23," he said.

McLauglin decided to retire about the time the legislature moved to realign the judicial districts in Kansas. "The towns in Marshall County have stayed about the same size. The decrease has come from the farm population which has moved to the cities," he said. "I was 68 years old and I couldn't see driving 100 miles each way to Troy over in Doniphan County to try cases. It was time for someone younger to take over."

Another change in the judicial system was the complexity of the trials, with the laws "giving more and more protection for the accused." But McLauglin thinks the pendulum is beginning to swing back now and more consideration will be given to the victims.

"The law is a search for the facts and the truth," he explained, but much time is taken up because "lots of foolish lawsuits are filed." However, he added, new laws have made it easier to settle more cases out of court and that "saves taxpayers a lot of money."

The demand for McLauglin's judicial expertise in the Kansas courtroom will probably continue as long as he is willing to take temporary assignments. But he doesn't mind having the time for other pursuits. Retirement has given him time to travel and watch his granddaughters grow up. He looks forward to warm weather and his daily round of golf with old friends. His other hobby is growing roses and today he maintains about 100 bushes in his backyard. Mornings are spent reading the *Topeka Daily Capital* and the *Kansas City Star and Times*. Afterwards, he says, he and his wife "settle the affairs of the world and have a second cup of coffee."

JUDITH MACKEY

Judith Mackey paints what she knows best—the Flint Hills of Kansas. The rolling tallgrass prairie in the east-central part of the state provides the background for the landscapes and scenes she portrays.

A native of Hutchinson, Mackey, along with her husband, Ken, and their three children, moved to Cottonwood Falls in 1972. Since 1978 the Mackeys have resided in a self-designed house on a bluff overlooking the Cottonwood Valley, about 12 miles west of Emporia. Mackey likes the relaxed living and open spaces and much of the subject matter for her oils can be seen from her house.

A self-taught artist, Mackey began painting in the early 1960s. "People had seen some things I had painted and they would ask me to paint something for them. The first year I just copied work and then I began using a color wheel and painting what I saw," Mackey explained. Her early work sold for $15 or $20. When it was suggested that she put a higher price tag on a painting she responded, "No one will ever pay $100 for my paintings." But they did. "I was shocked," Mackey recalled. Today her oils sell for $150 to $1,200, depending upon the size. A Mackey hangs in the office of U.S. Senator Robert Dole and her work has been exhibited throughout the United States and in Europe. Mackey's paintings have appeared on magazine covers and on greeting cards.

Mackey says it takes about 30 minutes to set the mood for a painting. The weather never deters her from working. In all seasons she paints the cottonwood trees along spring-fed draws, abandoned and working ranches, cattle, leather-faced cowboys astride their quarter horses, storms and skies, and hills with outcroppings of limestone. Recently on her easel was the Chase County Courthouse, the oldest in Kansas, built in 1871-1873 in the French Renaissance-style with a mansard roof, dormer windows, and a cupola. At the turn of the century a horse-drawn trolley ran from the courthouse to the neighboring town of Strong City, and Mackey has depicted that era in her new series of paintings.

Lindsborg celebrates its Swedish heritage with annual festivals of folk dancing and traditional arts and crafts. Courtesy, Unicorn Stock Photos

During the winter of 1987, Mackey wanted to paint a range scene in the snow. "It was 13 degrees and snowing. It was so cold my oils ran but I had the mood in about one-half hour and filled in later," she explained.

In retrospect Mackey believes she should have gone to school when she discovered she had some artistic talent. She says she's a lot more particular about her finished product today and that she might have reached that point sooner with instruction. Since 1984 she's been passing on what she's learned to her neighbors, conducting art classes in her studio basement. "I can teach my students in a few weeks what it took me a year to learn on my own," she said.

Mackey once traveled to shows throughout the western part of the United States but now limits herself to only a few. Her favorite is the juried art show held in conjunction with the American Royal, a rodeo, livestock, and horse show held every fall in Kansas City which attracts people from across the nation. In 1987 she took seven paintings to the show and sold all but one. Her work can also be purchased through galleries in Manhattan and Lindsborg, and at her own shop, Flint Hills Studio & Gallery in Cottonwood Falls.

MARY REIFF HUNKELER

Today when a community service organization needs a capable person to head a fund-raising drive or organize a group of volunteers, a name that often comes to mind is that of Mary Reiff Hunkeler. Since 1973 she has dedicated herself to the role of volunteer much as other people make a commitment to an employer. It's a role she enjoys and one that she finds full of challenge and satisfaction.

Hunkeler grew up in Kansas City, Missouri, and graduated from the University of Kansas School of Nursing. While working as a surgical nurse at the KU Medical Center, she met her husband, Dr. John Hunkeler, an ophthalmologist. The Hunkelers lived in California during John's internship and military service and then returned home in 1970. They elected to reside in Johnson County, first in Fairway

Citizens of Kansas have a deep sense of community responsibility: when it comes to volunteering their time to raise money, as these Harmon Boosters are doing, you can count on them to help. Photo by Bev Rehkop. Courtesy, Unicorn Stock Photos

and later in Mission Woods, where they have lived since 1976.

Hunkeler's career as a volunteer began with an invitation to a fund-raising event for the Crippled Children's Nursery School Association, an auxiliary of volunteers who provide assistance to teachers at the school. The nursery school serves handicapped children in Wyandotte and Johnson counties as well as those from other parts of the metropolitan Kansas City area. At the time, Hunkeler had put the nursing profession aside to raise her daughter, Amy, now a student at Harvard University.

"Amy was a preschooler and I knew how much time it took just mothering a normal child that age," Hunkeler explained. "I had empathy for the parents of these children with handicaps. I felt I needed to do something to help, to assist in providing care and training for their children and by volunteering at the nursery school I could contribute and make their family life a little easier."

Hunkeler offers her time as well as her organizational skills and expertise to many community groups, especially those concerned with children and health and family services.

From working directly with the children at the nursery school, she has gone on to serve as president of the volunteers association and president of its managing board, which concerns itself more with personnel, finances, public relations, and leadership building. She also has served as president of the Kansas City Junior League and currently sits on the boards of the Greater Kansas City Red Cross, University of Missouri at Kansas City Family Study Center, and the American Royal.

In the summer of 1988 Hunkeler chaired the Children's Mercy Hospital Golf Classic, a fund-raising event founded by professional golfer Tom Watson in 1980. A resident of Johnson County, Watson wanted to pay back the community for the support he has received through the years. Proceeds from the one-day charity exhibition, which involves about 500 volunteers, are used to enhance critical care services at the hospital.

Hunkeler and her husband have different volunteer interests in the community, but they support each other's involvements. Dr. Hunkeler's pet project is the Kansas City Eye Bank, which works like a clearinghouse between organ donors and physicians with patients in need of eye tissue.

The number of meetings Hunkeler attends as a full-time volunteer vary, but she says they range between three and six per week. In addition there is correspondence and other paperwork which she does at home.

Hunkeler believes an ongoing commitment is vital. "If I like the agency I'll give them longevity," she said. It's that longevity that Hunkeler fears may be subsiding as a younger generation of volunteers comes along. "Today's young people are cause-oriented and they are not attracted to these ongoing institutions in the community," she related.

Another concern Hunkeler has is that the burden of hands-on volunteer work has usually fallen on women and "they have less discretionary time than in the past. They are much more selective about where they spend their time."

One way Hunkeler hopes to encourage younger people to take an interest in volunteerism is the approach she used with her daughter. During high school Amy spent Saturdays working as a hospital volunteer. During the summer of 1987, prior to entering Harvard, she spent 20 hours per week working in a thrift shop. Both exposures, Hunkeler believes, were "positive experiences."

Hunkeler hastens to add that being a volunteer doesn't have to involve the kind of time she puts in. "If you bake cookies for your children's fourth-grade class at Halloween, that's volunteerism."

BILL HATFIELD

Mention that you come from Dodge City to strangers and they'll probably look down at your sides to see if you're toting a six-shooter, or at the very least, wonder if you're using a horse as your major form of transportation.

That's because more than a century ago, for about 10 years, this southwestern Kansas town was a major railhead for the Texas cattle drives, attracting cowboys and buffalo hunters as well as a motley crowd anxious to relieve any and all folks of their money. The respectable citizenry hired lawmen like Wyatt Earp and Bat Masterson to keep the peace, and the events of those days have been embellished for books, movies, and television.

Like most of the city's 18,000 residents, Bill Hatfield chuckles at the notion that Dodge is still the wild West. He doesn't mind, he just chuckles.

Hatfield was born in Dodge City and, except for a time at the University of Kansas, has always lived here. His roots run deep. His great-grandparents came to Kansas in a covered wagon in the 1880s and took up farming. His grandfather, Mahlon Ogden, still operates that farm, which is located between Kinsley and Greensburg. His father, R.W. Hatfield, is a pharmacist at the Prescription Center in Dodge City and his mother, Connie Hatfield, works there as well. He married his high school sweetheart, Lynette Riedlinger. Today Hatfield is a science teacher at Dodge City High School, and Lynette teaches kindergarten at Northwest Elementary School.

Hatfield admits he fell into the role of educator. After leaving KU, he returned to Dodge City and graduated from St. Mary of the Plains College with a B.S. in biology. When it came time to do his student teaching he did so under his former

June Bell, on far left, takes her nursery school class to the courthouse in Cottonwood Falls for a Halloween treat. Photo by Arni Katz

biology teacher at Dodge City High School, Tom Keeley. Hatfield thought briefly about leaving Dodge to teach in another part of the state, but before he could seriously consider anything else the local board of education offered him a contract.

Today Hatfield teaches biology, anatomy, zoology, and senior honors biology. Having been on both sides of the desk at the local high school has given him insight into the way education has evolved in the state. "When I was in school about three-fifths of the students came from the farm. Now I don't have more than one or two in a class," he said.

Hatfield thinks maybe the students are a little more ambitious than they were 10 years ago. "They are highly motivated. They're interested in making excellent grades and very competitive about getting into the college of their choice," he explained.

But Hatfield's commitment to the high school doesn't end in the classroom. When the Dodge City Red Demons play football, he usually runs up and down the field with the chains. During basketball season he helps out with scorekeeping. Like many of the residents of this southwestern Kansas community, he loves to cheer on the home team.

"We're small enough for the whole town to rally behind the team," Hatfield said, pointing out that Dodge likes to play teams from larger towns like Wichita and Lawrence.

When the hometown team isn't playing and during vacations, the Hatfields like to travel—although that has been curtailed somewhat since the birth of their daughter, Emily.

"We go to Kansas City once in a while but more often like to spend the weekend in Wichita," he said. Wichita is 150 miles east of Dodge and offers the shopping, restaurants, and other attractions of a metropolitan area that draw the Hatfields and other residents of western Kansas. Would Hatfield trade his life in a small Kansas town for the big city? He says that might happen someday, but right now Dodge is where he wants to be.

LEON TRAMMELL

It's easy to tell after a simple hello that Leon Trammell hails not from Kansas but from one of her southern neighbors. And Kansas can be grateful that after his graduation from Arkansas' Valley Springs High School in 1950, Trammell decided not to accept the scholarship he had been offered in animal husbandry at the University of Arkansas.

"I couldn't see spending the rest of my life as a dairy farmer. My brother-in-law had a job in Wichita's aircraft industry and I decided to come north and try to get on at one of the plants," Trammell recalled.

Trammell worked for Boeing for a couple of years and then joined his family in a construction business in Hominy, Oklahoma. He returned to Wichita in 1954 and went to work for the Kansas Milling Co., where he learned a lot about the grain business, particularly about the maintenance of and capital improvements on elevators. He learned enough, in fact, to found his own company—Tramco—in 1964.

The business began in a building which Trammell rented for $15 a month. Today the company has 80 employees and Trammell predicted that sales in 1990 would top $10 million.

Trammell started Tramco because he saw a need for a company which could service the grain elevators and feed mills that dot the landscape in the Midwest. But it was the antiquated conveyor system used by these businesses that put Tramco where it is today.

"Anywhere they move grain or free-flowing material they need a conveyor system," Trammell explained. "The enmass conveyor was invented in England in the 1920s but never improved. I talked to everyone who had one and asked them how they would make it better."

He found out how to do just that, purchased the necessary patents, and developed an updated and improved enmass conveyor. In addition to moving materials efficiently it also reduces and restricts air pollutants such as grain dust.

Although only 10 percent of Tramco's business is in Kansas, Trammell believes it is the right place to be located. "There's no competition within 100 miles and Wichita is the ideal location for this type of company," he said.

Most of the grain produced in the United States is grown within an area 700 miles west and east of the Missouri River, from southern Canada to Texas. Wichita is located about 200 miles southwest of where the Missouri River turns east and flows across the state of Missouri into the Mississippi River. As Trammell points out, anywhere bread is eaten, grain must be stored and conveyed. That means Tramco conveyors have found their way into the 48 contiguous states as well as 23 foreign countries. Today sales of Tramco conveyors are not limited to the grain business. Companies which move other free-flowing materials such as ash and coal use them as well.

Trammell says his wanderlust may have been responsible for the creation of

Tramco's international department. He's quick to point out that dealing with foreign buyers is much different than domestic sales. For example, many foreign companies prefer the involvement of government officials. "Their initial presence adds credibility," Trammell said.

In 1986 Trammell was part of a Kansas delegation led by Governor John Carlin to look at agricultural areas of the People's Republic of China. "I never dreamed when I was growing up in northwest Arkansas that I would have the opportunity to travel to so many countries and be exposed to so many people. You get a much truer feeling for a people and their culture when you meet them in circumstances other than as a tourist," said Trammell.

It was on one of these trips abroad that Trammell met his wife, Jeri. Since their marriage in January 1988, he has stayed closer to home and turned much of the international marketing over to the sales staff. He says he's become a homebody. He's also become a rancher. The Trammells live on a 2,500-acre ranch east of Wichita. They have 650 head of cattle, a family of cats, and two dogs, Jake and Lovey.

Like the teacher, artist, volunteer, jurist, and thousands of other Kansans whose names go unmentioned on these pages, Leon Trammell, his wife, and family make a priceless contribution to the state of Kansas—they give it heart.

This farmer, seen taking a break in his barn in Hutchinson, is among many in Kansas who have made the state number one in wheat production. Photo by Jeff Hetler. Courtesy, Unicorn Stock Photos

This is one of the four French cannons that are located in Fort Leavenworth. Cast in 1774 in Paris, no one knows exactly how they came to the fort. Photo by Arni Katz

2

PLACES AND PASTIMES

Kansas might be called a place of discovery for visitors as well as residents. It seems like every county has some diversion to offer, ranging from outdoor recreation to museums of the past, present, and future. Seasonally there are community celebrations and special events. Those seeking a different living experience can try the Kansas version of a dude ranch or spend a few days traveling by covered wagon like the pioneers.

Like a lot of native Kansans as well as newcomers, Kay Calhoun Mehrer has engaged in a love affair with the Flint Hills part of the state all of her life. This 50-mile tract through east-central Kansas is the only extensive unplowed bluestem or tallgrass prairie remaining in the United States. Because of its steep slopes and shallow upland soil, the area did not lend itself to cultivation. One thing it does lend itself to is relaxation.

Mehrer fondly remembers growing up in Emporia and spending weekends with family and friends at Lake Kahola, about 20 miles northwest of town. She could never quite separate herself from this Flint Hills retreat. Residents of Fairway in Johnson County, Mehrer and her husband, Chuck, purchased a small cabin on the lake in 1988. Now they join other Kansans in one of the state's most popular weekend pastimes—getting away to the parks, lakes, and recreation areas which dot the landscape.

Many of the old cabins surrounding Lake Kahola have been leveled and replaced with modern structures, but the Mehrers

wanted to keep things simple. They put aluminum siding on the outside of the cabin, made only necessary repairs, hired someone to mow the grass, and stocked essentials. They spend as much time there as possible. Although the cabin has only one bedroom, an enclosed sleeping porch and a hideaway bed provide accommodations for eight people.

"We go down to relax. It's a beautiful setting and it's peaceful. I like to look at the clear sky and the stars, take walks and maybe take the old boat out for a row around the lake," she said.

That search for peacefulness led Jane Koger, of the Homestead Ranch near Matfield Green in the Flint Hills, to invite other women to sample prairie life. On the 6,000-acre working cattle ranch, guests are encouraged to go horseback riding or help round up the livestock, feed the chickens, and work in the fields and gardens. They can learn about wildflowers, quilting, local history, and the prairie ecosystem. Women can spend from two to five days at the ranch during May, June, and September.

LEFT: Colorful sugar maple leaves provide a picturesque fall landscape. Photo by Arni Katz

FACING PAGE: This peaceful scene is from Leavenworth State Fishing Lake near Tonganoxie. Photo by Keith Philpott

A map reader would need a keen eye to spot these Flint Hills retreats. For example, Lake Kahola straddles the boundaries of Morris and Chase counties halfway between Emporia and Council Grove. There are many small lakes like this throughout the state as well as 25 federal reservoirs, which offer boating, swimming, fishing, camping, picnicking, and hiking. Cedar Bluff, El Dorado, and Melvern are the three largest and Tuttle Creek offers the most shoreline. Milford is the largest man-made lake in the state. There are also 48 state fishing lakes and nearly 100 community lakes.

Canoe enthusiasts will find 10 river trails which have been routed by the Kansas Canoe Association in cooperation with the Kansas Park & Resources Authority. They vary in skill required, length of trip, and camping opportunities.

Other sports-minded people look forward to autumn and hunting season. Besides pheasants and bobwhite quails, there are mourning doves, turkeys, ducks, geese, coyotes, deer, rabbits, and squirrels. The Kansas Fish and Game Commission

APOLLO 11

manages 69 wildlife areas, encompassing more than 200,000 acres, where public hunting is permitted. Another eight wildlife areas are managed by the federal government.

OLD-TIME ADVENTURES

For a different type of outdoor experience, the person seeking adventure can sign up for the Flint Hills Overland Wagon Train Trip. The grueling, endless days endured by the pioneers have been condensed into a 24-hour trip, traveling by covered wagon, stagecoach, or horse. Four trips covering about six miles are planned per year for between 40 and 50 passengers plus a crew of 15.

"We refer to ourselves as weekend pioneers," says El Dorado attorney Ervin E. Grant, one of the organizers of the trips. Sleeping facilities are available in four covered wagons and the rest of the participants must bring their own tents and bedrolls. Four meals are served, three of them over a campfire. Grant says people come from throughout the United States to sample the pioneer life. The cost of the adventure for a family of four is approximately $300.

Like the covered wagon trips, there are many attractions in Kansas which satisfy man's fascination with the old West and stimulate the imagination about how frontier people lived.

The Santa Fe Trail was the first broad mark made by civilization across the face of the prairies. The trail was 775 miles long, and 500 of those miles were in Kansas. There are remnants of the wagon ruts preserved throughout the state, although defining those ruts requires a healthy imagination because in most places the trail was 60 to 100 feet wide.

One place for viewing the trail is a 40-acre piece of pastureland four miles southwest of Fort Larned. A farmer by the name of Paul Eikmeier recognized the historical significance of this area and left it in its native state. Today the tract is administered by the National Park Service. Somewhat disguised by a blanket of native grasses and a prairie-dog town, there are nevertheless five distinct sets of ruts.

Upon close observation it also is possible to see the old buffalo wallows, although the mighty herds disappeared a century ago. These wallows now appear as round or oval-shaped depressions six to eight feet in diameter. The bison would roll for a dust or mud bath as temporary relief from biting flies. The wallows also provided natural watering holes for birds, animals, and men after sudden prairie thunderstorms.

MILITARY LEGACIES

There isn't a more authentic preservation in the state than Fort Larned itself. Located six miles west of the town with the same name, the fort served as a military outpost from 1859 until 1878. Standing in the middle of the grassy parade ground, surrounded by sandstone buildings, visitors have only to close their eyes and listen for the cavalry to come riding up or imagine the commanding officer talking to the troops from the porch of his quarters.

The National Park Service has furnished two enlisted men's barracks; the post hospital, bakery, blacksmith's shop, and officers' quarters; storehouses; and blockhouses. Plans also call for the rebuilding of the sutler's store, which was a combination general store, restaurant, and recreation hall for residents as well as

FACING PAGE, TOP: Avid boaters take advantage of Lake Shawnee in Topeka. Photo by Rod Furgason. Courtesy, Unicorn Stock Photos

FACING PAGE, BELOW LEFT: A proud young fisherman shows off his catch. Photo by Bev Rehkop. Courtesy, Unicorn Stock Photos

FACING PAGE, BELOW RIGHT: Quail, deer, and pheasant are among the various game available to the hunting enthusiast. Photo by John Ebeling. Courtesy, Unicorn Stock Photos

visitors to the fort. Almost as interesting as the fort itself, although park superintendent Maurice Ross would disagree, is the graffiti which was carved into the sandstone by three generations of area residents. Now the U.S. government warns against such behavior with a sign which reads, "For many years it was considered sport to carve one's name upon this fort. It is now preserved as a national park so enjoy yourself, but don't make your mark."

Between the fort and town is another adjunct to the pioneer history in the area. This is the Santa Fe Trail Center, a museum which displays not only a covered wagon but other influences along the route. Included are prehistoric Indian artifacts, a Wichita Indian grass lodge, a full-size mounted buffalo, pioneer church displays, early musical instruments, and a series of rooms showing pioneer life in the early 1900s. Outdoor exhibits include a sod house, dugout home, limestone cooling house, one-room schoolhouse, and a Santa Fe Railroad depot. The center also provides a research library and archives.

Above: Pictured here is the U.S. Army Command and General Staff College, where only the highest ranking officials attend from all over the world. Photo by Arni Katz

Like Fort Larned, military outposts in the state played an important part in the nation's westward expansion. Fort Scott, in the southeast part of the state, was established in 1842 as a garrison for peacekeeping efforts on the Indian frontier. During the Civil War, Fort Scott became the base of operations for many border skirmishes over the slavery issue. Today the fort is a National Historic Site administered by the National Park Service. About half of the fort's original stone and frame buildings have been restored and the rest have been reconstructed. Local residents re-create life at the fort during special weekends from May to October. Adjacent to the military post is Fort Scott's downtown, a three-block-long area where buildings have been preserved with painstaking care. Throughout the town, homes, churches, and other edifices have been restored to their Victorian splendor.

Two other Kansas military posts, Fort Leavenworth, established in 1827, and Fort Riley, dating from 1853, are still active installations.

Today Fort Leavenworth is the home of the U.S. Army Command and General Staff College, a senior tactical school for advanced military education which attracts military personnel from around the world. The "Main Parade," the original center of the post, has been beautifully preserved and near it is the Rookery, the oldest continually occupied home in the state. Built in 1832, it was the residence of the first territorial governor, and General Douglas MacArthur lived there in the early 1900s.

Fort Riley spreads out over 100,000 acres near Manhattan and is headquarters for the First Infantry Division, nicknamed the "Big Red One." In the original part of the fort are native limestone buildings which include the U.S. Cavalry Museum. The museum traces the history of the American horse soldier from the Revolutionary War until 1950, when the cavalry branch of the service ceased to exist. On display are uniforms, headgear, and saddles as well as dioramas depicting the role of cavalrymen in the defense of the country. The sculpture and picture gallery features

ABOVE: Fort Scott, in the southeast part of the state, served during the Civil War as a base station for border disputes waged over the slavery issue and for keeping peace between the settlers and Indians. Photo by Robert VanKirk. Courtesy, Unicorn Stock Photos

LEFT: Designated as a National Historic Site, Fort Scott has been completely restored and is administered by the National Park Service. Photo by Robert VanKirk. Courtesy, Unicorn Stock Photos

works by Frederic Remington and other artists. Near the museum, the fort maintains a small herd of bison.

WHERE HISTORY LIVES

Much of this country's story of westward expansion is told in Kansas, not only in visits to the military outposts but to the city and county museums as well.

A re-creation of Wichita during the late 1800s, known as "Cowtown," is located on the banks of the Arkansas River in Wichita's Sim Memorial Park and features 36 buildings on 17 acres. Among them are Wichita's first permanent house, a church, a drugstore, a blacksmith shop, a saloon, a newspaper office, and a jail.

High Plains Museum in Goodland houses America's first patented helicopter, prehistoric fossils, and Indian artifacts along with pioneer toys and dolls, farming tools, and implements. The Chisholm Trail Museum in Wellington has 42 rooms of displays with more than 12,000 exhibits.

The most comprehensive museum is located eight miles west of downtown Topeka and is operated by the Kansas State Historical Society. The Kansas Museum of History, which moved to its new location in 1984, traces the people and events in the state from Indian settlements to current times. Newly completed is the Atchison, Topeka and Santa Fe Railway exhibit, which features the engine, coal and water car, business car, and drovers car. Dorothy's Rainbow Diner is a popular display that focuses on the eating habits of people as well as on food items which originated in the state. Included is a neon sign from the first McDonald's restaurant in Topeka.

The museum's collection is further enhanced by a full-scale replica of a grass lodge like those built by the Wichita Indians, a buffalo hide tepee, a furnished log house, and a discovery room where visitors can experiment with objects such as a treadle sewing machine. In addition to its permanent collection, the museum features fascinating "temporary" displays that are changed every three to four months.

Kansas is proud of its colorful past, and much has been done to preserve that

Southwest of Manhattan, Fort Riley is currently the home of the First Infantry Division. Having once served as headquarters for the U.S. Cavalry, the fort now contains the U.S. Cavalry Museum. Photo by Arni Katz

The Place of Meditation is the final resting place of Dwight D. Eisenhower, Mamie Doud Eisenhower, and their son Doud Dwight Eisenhower. Photo by Mark E. Gibson

heritage for future generations. Another legacy of the state has been that of Dwight David Eisenhower, supreme commander of the Allied armies in Europe during World War II and president of the United States from 1953 to 1961.

Eisenhower grew up in a simple frame house near the railroad tracks in Abilene. He played football for Abilene High School and worked in a local creamery before being admitted to West Point. His mother, Ida, grew fruit and vegetables to supplement the family's meager income. Today that boyhood home and its surrounding 22 acres comprise part of the Eisenhower Center. The house contains original family furnishings and the life and times of the 34th president can be traced in the adjacent museum. Among the exhibits are gifts from foreign countries to the Eisenhowers, a collection of quilts made by his mother, military staff cars, and thousands of other mementos of his life. Another building houses a library which contains presidential papers and has research facilities for scholars. The Eisenhowers and a son who died at the age of three are buried in the Place of Meditation.

SIGHTS TO SEE

Presidents, pioneers, cowboys, and other such heroes have always stimulated people's imaginations and curiosity, but a more modern-day hero has taken hold of

TOPEKA'S
FAMILY
FAVORITE
McDonald's
JOHN SILVER'S
Vista
RESTAURANTS
White Castle
SONIC
Kentucky Fried Chicken
Taco Grande
TACO BELL
Hardee's
A&W
TACO CASA
BIG CHEESE PIZZA
BURGER KING
Dairy Queen
Coca-Cola

Kansans, especially the younger generation. Today's hero is the astronaut, especially the three from Kansas. Ron Evans, a native of St. Francis and a graduate of Topeka public schools and the University of Kansas, commanded the pilot ship during the Apollo 17 flight to the moon. Joe Engle, a Chapman native, commanded the Space Shuttle *Columbia*'s second mission. Steve Hawley, born in Ottawa and raised in Salina, was a mission specialist aboard the maiden flight of the Space Shuttle *Discovery*. The lives of the three are profiled in exhibits at the Kansas Cosmosphere and Space Center, located on the Hutchinson Community College campus. The center receives more than 350,000 visitors annually. On display are more than $100 million worth of spacesuits and other artifacts. There are "hands on" exhibits and an astronaut data bank. The Carey Omnimax Theater utilizes a 44-foot tilted dome and six-channel stereo sound system to bring seasonal films to viewers. Because of the popularity of this program, reservations are advisable. The center also includes a planetarium and live sky lectures are presented on weekends.

BELOW: Artifacts on display at the Kansas Cosmosphere and Space Center include numerous spacesuits and spacecraft. Photo by Ron Welch

Nearly every visitor of junior high age dreams of attending the Future Astronaut Training Program, a five-day summer camp experience held at the center. Each day different aspects of space flight are taught. The schedule of training builds toward the final day, when students use their newly acquired knowledge to conduct a simulated space shuttle mission.

Another favorite of Kansas' young people as well as their parents and grandparents is the Sedgwick County Zoo, located seven miles northwest of downtown Wichita. The zoo was opened in 1971, replacing a smaller one in Riverside Park. Today the zoo has a specimen count of 1,400 on 212 acres and averages 300,000 visitors annually. The Zoological Society has 3,000 members and most of them have family memberships. Animals can be petted at the Children's Farm, and the zoo's Herpetarium displays desert, nocturnal, aquatic, and other reptiles. In the Jungle, heat and humidity create a natural habitat for exotic plants, birds, and other animals. (Walk carefully, though, because the creatures here are used to humans and will cross right in front of people on the footpath.) Elephants, baboons, giraffes, lions, and hippos live in the African Veldt. The Pampas-Outback resembles the wild regions of South America and Australia, and the chimpanzees and orangutans keep themselves as well as visitors entertained in the Man and Ape exhibit.

FACING PAGE: A popular display at the Kansas Museum of History is Dorothy's Rainbow Diner, which includes a neon sign from the first McDonald's restaurant in Topeka. Photo by Bob Barrett

THE KANSAS STATE FAIR

The Cosmosphere and Space Center is not the only attraction in Hutchinson, which has been the home of the Kansas State Fair for more than 75 years. In an article for *Smithsonian* magazine, author Noel Perrin described the Kansas State Fair as "one of the most thoroughly American." Perrin claims to have several criteria for judging a fair's value, and one is food. He raved about the chicken with noodles and home-baked raisin pie served by members of the South Hutchinson United

The annual Flint Hills Rodeo gives Kansas cowboys the chance to show off their best stuff. Photo by Bob Barrett

Methodist Church. No one need ever go hungry at the Kansas State Fair, for church booths serving everything from tacos to pancakes are as much a part of the 10-day September extravaganza as the stock car races, tractor pulls, and 4-H fashion shows.

And there are always those attractions that bespeak the times. The first fair featured entries in such categories as homemade shoes, quinces, and currant and grape wines. In 1919 tanks and field artillery used in World War I were displayed on the fairgrounds. Around 1950 Continental Trailways showed off the latest in buses and provided a place for weary fairgoers to rest their feet. Today foreign exhibits are popular. No matter what the trend, there's bound to be something for everyone. Perrin said when he visited the Kansas State Fair he counted 172 different modes of entertainment.

KANSAS FESTIVITIES

The state fair may be the headline special event in the state, but everywhere there are seasonal festivals and events.

On Shrove Tuesday the town of Liberal competes with Olney, England, in the International Pancake Day Race. Female competitors wearing housedresses, aprons, and head scarves run an S-shaped course, carrying skillets and flipping their pancakes twice. The women of Olney have been racing for five centuries; the race came to Liberal in 1949. To date, the score is Olney, 20; Liberal, 19; and one tie.

An Indian Peace Treaty Pageant takes place every three years in Medicine Lodge. A cast of 1,000 presents the pageant in memory of peace treaties negotiated in 1867 by the United States with five hostile Plains Indian tribes.

The biggest annual attraction in Independence is Neewollah, which is

Halloween spelled backwards. It began as a nighttime parade in 1919 to provide for a sane and safe Halloween. Today it is a four-day observance, with schools, lodges, churches, and the business community participating. Besides the parade, Neewollah includes a carnival, concerts, and dances.

Even outlaws are remembered. Coffeyville reenacts the infamous Dalton raid each October. The 1892 attempted bank robbery left all but one of the gang dead as well as four citizens. Also in October is the Biblesta in Humboldt, an annual parade portraying biblical scenes on floats.

In September, Winfield hosts the Bluegrass Festival and National Flat-Pick Guitar Championships. Caldwell sponsors the Great Land Rush Bicycle Race. Paola has a chili cook-off. Arkansas City celebrates with the Cherokee Strip B-B-Q and Pioneer Festival. There are quilt shows, rodeos, arts and crafts fairs, Christmas parades and bazaars, and numerous other events throughout the state which mark the seasons or just give folks a reason to get together and have a good time.

Kansans are a social people and that dates back to the pioneer days. In *Pioneer Women*, Joanna Stratton says settlers found many forms of amusement besides dancing, riding, and picnicking (all common pastimes today). She mentions "winter sleigh rides across snowy fields, taffy pulls in warm kitchens, and group spelling bees in the local schoolhouse."

Probably the greatest institution in the entire state, though, is morning coffee. Whether it takes place at the DonDo in Larned, Waid's in Prairie Village, the Corner Cafe in Garnett, or any other favorite gathering spot, the important topics of the day—politics, weather, prices, health, happiness, and what's up with the neighbors—are covered.

The Hieberts perform at a dulcimer festival in Overland Park. Photo by Keith Philpott

Cheerleaders spark excitement at the big game between the University of Kansas Jayhawks and the Kansas State University Wildcats. Photo by Arni Katz

3

LEARNING AND LIVING

Persons searching for quality education, health care, and neighborhoods find that the state of Kansas offers all three. Probably the best place to begin discovering that quality is in the state's higher education system. Excellence here has had a domino effect on other aspects of living.

There are more than 65 institutions of higher learning in the state, and the majority of students attend one of the six state universities governed by the nine-member Board of Regents. There are nearly 80,000 students attending the state universities, which have nearly 5,000 faculty members. Regents chairman Richard Dodderidge points out that most Kansas high school graduates go to state schools, and that Kansas is one of only two states in the nation that does not have qualified admissions. Any Kansas resident with a high school degree may enroll. The Board of Regents has authority over all aspects of the schools except for public funding, which is determined by the state legislature. Dodderidge says the board's primary objective through 1991 is to acquire additional funding for hiring and retaining top faculty.

KU

Only 12 cities in the state have populations exceeding the enrollment at the University of Kansas in Lawrence of nearly 27,000 students. Located about a 45-minute drive west of Kansas City, KU's 1,000-acre campus sits atop Mount Oread, a limestone ridge overlooking the Kansas and Wakarusa river valleys. The

The University of Kansas in Lawrence is the largest school in the educational system and offers a wide range of graduate and undergraduate degrees, including law and medicine. Courtesy, Unicorn Stock Photos

beautiful red-roofed limestone buildings which line the main street of the campus, Jayhawk Boulevard, are visible for miles outside the city. The newer buildings on campus blend well with the older architecture. Students come to "the hill" from all 50 states and 100 foreign countries, although the majority are Kansas residents.

There are many reasons why KU attracts so many students, not the least of which is that it provides high-quality education at a reasonable cost. Academics are tough here, with strict distribution requirements depending upon the course of study. Eleven of KU's 14 academic schools are open to undergraduates. KU has the only medical and pharmacy schools in the state and one of two law schools. In the last quarter-century, KU has produced Rhodes scholars at a rate of nearly one a year and has ranked in the top 15 in the nation among universities enrolling National Merit Scholars. More than 90 percent of the full-time faculty have earned the highest degree in their fields, and most teach at the undergraduate level. Through private support, the university has brought more than 50 nationally and internationally recognized scholars to campus to serve as distinguished professors.

KU's William Allen White School of Journalism is consistently ranked as one of the best in the United States. Excellence in news reporting and editorial writing remains at the heart of the journalism school, but KU also offers programs in advertising, magazine writing, photojournalism, and broadcasting. Students supplement classroom studies with work on the student newspaper, the *University Daily Kansan;* the school magazine, the *Jayhawk Journalist;* three on-campus radio stations, KJHK, KFKU, and KANU; and closed-circuit television facilities. Admission to the school of journalism does not take place until the junior year.

The School of Architecture and Urban Design admits freshmen to its five-year program on a limited basis. KU is listed as one of the American Institute of Architects' top 15 schools in the nation. The School of Fine Arts also admits freshmen and offers the only art and design program in Kansas. It also is the only institution authorized by the Board of Regents to offer doctoral degrees in music.

Programs in the School of Education are aimed at students preparing for work in education-related fields as well as those who are striving to become educators in elementary and secondary schools. A bachelor's degree is awarded at the end of four years, but a fifth year must be completed to achieve certification. In addition to the previously mentioned schools, degrees also are granted from the College of Liberal Arts and Sciences; schools of allied health, business, engineering, social welfare, and nursing; and the Graduate School.

Sports have always been important at this Big Eight Conference school, which competes with Kansas State University and six other universities from Oklahoma, Colorado, Nebraska, Iowa, and Missouri. Sports immortals Wilt Chamberlain, Jim Ryun, Gale Sayers, and John Riggins are among those who started their careers here. The newest additions to KU's roster of sports heroes are the members of the 1987-88 basketball team and their coach, Larry Brown. They did what everyone said couldn't be done and won the national championship at the NCAA Final Four held in April 1988 in Kansas City.

In addition to the players, no KU sporting event would be complete without three important accoutrements—the Jayhawk, Rock Chalk, and waving wheat.

KU's Jayhawk mascot—a large, endearing, bright-blue bird with a mop of red hair, a yellow beak, and yellow shoes—is unique to the school. The exact origin of the term Jayhawk is unclear, although most people agree that it stems from the nickname given Kansas Free Staters by pro-slavery forces in the late 1850s. The term gained respect and became a symbol of courage and strength, and in 1912 a student named Henry Maloy drew a cartoon character which he called a Jayhawk.

The creature has since gone through six versions, the current emblem having been created in 1946 by Hal Sandy, an advertising major in the school of journalism. Sandy created a smiling, friendly Jayhawk to replace the fighting Jayhawk which had been used during the war years. Now a designer and a resident of Westwood Hills, Sandy says of his Jayhawk, "It was the only cartoon character I've ever drawn in my life." Sandy obtained a copyright on the bird and arranged to market decals through the newly opened KU bookstore. The bookstore later purchased the rights from him, and now Sandy's happy Jayhawk appears everywhere you find a KU student or alumnus.

Two friends stop to chat between classes at KU. Photo by Arni Katz

Rock Chalk is part of a chant that is yelled at KU sporting events. Originally replacing "rah, rah" in the school cheer 100 years ago, the words

BELOW: *This quarterback sets up the next play at the big game between the Jayhawks and the Wildcats. Photo by Arni Katz*

are still used today as in "Rock Chalk, Jayhawk, KU." Along with the Jayhawk and the cheer is waving wheat, which is the act of swaying arms above heads in unison to celebrate touchdowns at football games and basketball victories. From a distance the motion resembles the waving wheat of the Kansas countryside.

K-STATE

Established in 1863, Kansas State University in Manhattan was the nation's original land-grant college and is now part of the state system.

Kansas State's mascot is a wildcat that is a little different from most, because it's purple. K-State is Purple Pride country, and everything from pom-poms to wallpaper has been designed with this in mind. K-State is a mega-university but smaller than KU, with 18,000 students on a 700-acre campus. The university owns or leases thousands of additional acres for agricultural experimentation.

ABOVE: These fans know only one cheer and that's for their team, the Kansas State University Wildcats. Photo by Arni Katz

RIGHT: This fan gets into the spirit of the homecoming game. Photo by Arni Katz

Through the Federal Land-Grant Act, K-State is responsible for all county extension activities in the state and is noted for its programs in agriculture, home economics, and veterinary medicine. The emphasis on these fields makes for some unique majors. Agricultural engineers design machinery and systems for efficient and economical production of food, feed, and fiber while maintaining a concern for the conservation of water and soil resources. Bakery science and management majors study the commercial baking industry. Before entering the College of Veterinary Medicine, successful candidates must complete a three-year minimum of preparatory courses at the undergraduate level. However, not all students pursue these fields. Many enroll in either the College of Arts and Sciences, College of Business Administration, College of Architecture and Design, College of Education, or College of Human Ecology.

Turner High School musicians know how to strike up the band. Photo by Bruce Mathews

transition from three-year junior high schools for grades seven through nine to two-year middle schools for grades seven and eight. Ninth graders now attend high school.

In an article published by *Town and Country* magazine, Shawnee Mission East High School was rated as one of America's top public high schools. The article said: "Shawnee Mission East is outstanding in a school district whose five high schools all rank above the national average. This Kansas City suburb attracts upper-middle class families that expect the best in public education."

Overall test scores rank the district in the 90th percentile. In 1984 ABC-TV featured Shawnee Mission in a television documentary on public schools across the nation. Recently Shawnee Mission South was one of seven high schools in the country cited as models of excellence. More than 80 percent of Shawnee Mission seniors enroll in college. Forty-five of the state's 164 National Merit scholarship semifinalists in 1987 were from Shawnee Mission schools. Faculty members with master's degrees total 70 percent.

National surveys like those which spotlighted the Shawnee Mission district often look primarily at test scores, the number of students enrolled in advanced placement courses, and how much clout the school has with selective colleges. But there are several other factors which make Shawnee Mission an excellent climate for learning. One is a faculty with longevity. Many of the teachers were working in the district before unification in 1969. To obtain a teaching contract in this district has always been considered a coup. In 1987 Shawnee Mission hired 184 new teachers.

Parent involvement also contributes to the district's success. One program sponsored by the East PTA is "College Clinic." Representatives from colleges and universities from around the country participate and provide information about their institutions. One night a year the school becomes a giant shopping mall for higher education, attracting not only students from Shawnee Mission but from throughout the metropolitan area as well.

As population in the Shawnee Mission district has stabilized, decreasing enrollments have caused some school closings in recent years. Another school district to the south tackles the opposite problem, keeping up with a burgeoning population. The Blue Valley district has more than 7,000 students and expects that number to double by 1993. Three more schools opened in 1989, bringing the total number of schools to 14.

THE MENNINGER FOUNDATION

Dr. Roy Menninger calls it a "beacon of hope." He's talking about the Menninger Foundation, which was founded by his grandfather, Dr. Charles F. Menninger, in 1925. Menninger's is known worldwide as one of the major psychiatric treatment and teaching facilities in the world. Charles Menninger had visited the Mayo Clinic in Rochester, Minnesota, in 1919 and he decided to found a similar institution in Topeka for the treatment of the mentally ill. It has been a guidepost for most of the psychiatric hospitals that have since been established in this country and many others around the world. Most people agree that because of Menninger's, the mentally ill have gained hope and a chance to escape incarceration.

Today the Menninger Foundation employs more than 1,200 persons and has an annual budget of $44 million, provided through fees, tuition, private contributions, and federal grants. Mental health care and treatment are still the cornerstone of Menninger's, and in 1987 the hospital treated 615 inpatients while its outpatient services cared for 12,000 persons. Employee Judy Craig emphasized the "beacon of hope" role played by Menninger's. "People come in sheer desperation. We get many of the most difficult patients who have treatment failures elsewhere," she said. Other programs at the hospital include education, research, application, and prevention.

Nearly 2,000 people have received training at Menninger's, and alumni practice in 50 states and 28 foreign countries. Besides psychiatric residencies for physicians, other fields of study include clinical psychology, clinical social work, pastoral care and counseling, occupational therapy, and specific psychiatric disciplines. Last year 2,000 persons participated in 35 workshops covering a variety of disciplines.

Research projects run the gamut of human needs. Currently researchers are exploring genetics to determine whether behavior can be passed from one generation to the next. They are looking at biofeedback as a method for controlling migraine headaches, hypertension, and psychosomatic illnesses. Also being studied are alcoholism and the nature of mental illness, specifically schizophrenia.

Menninger's has pioneered programs of prevention and the application of mental health know-how in industries, schools, churches, courts, and prisons. Seminars on the basic principles of human behavior help thousands of people in their day-to-day lives. One rehabilitation program assesses disabled persons and injured workers to determine their vocational abilities.

Menninger's welcomes visitors to its museum, housed in the Tower building modeled after Independence Hall in Philadelphia. In addition to a large collection of Sigmund Freud papers, there are exhibits tracing the history of the Menninger

Foundation's efforts to promote knowledge of mental illness. Dr. Karl Menninger, although in his late 90s, still drops in at the office occasionally and has the first reserved parking space in the lot behind the building. He has written many books which became best-sellers, not only for medical students but for the general public as well. His titles include *The Human Mind, The Crime of Punishment, Love Against Hate, Man Against Himself,* and *Whatever Became of Sin?*

THE INSTITUTE OF LOGOPEDICS

A few years after the founding of Menninger's, another Kansan pioneered in the health field. In 1934, under the leadership of Dr. Martin F. Palmer, the University of Wichita opened its Department of Speech Services which later became the Institute of Logopedics. Palmer, a specialist in communicative disorders, believed "a person's ability to communicate is paramount to leading a meaningful and productive life."

Founded in 1925 by Dr. Charles F. Menninger, the Menninger Foundation is considered to be one of the best in the nation when it comes to the treatment of the mentally ill. Photo by Denny Bailly. Courtesy, Unicorn Stock

The Institute of Logopedics emphasizes communication development in a program integrating educational, medical, and behavioral science services in one location. Plainly stated, the Institute of Logopedics helps children with multiple disabilities become independent members of society. Children learn to count money, tell time, and follow recipes. They learn to read job applications, bus schedules, and signs. Often their bodies must be trained as well as their minds and they are taught to walk, lace shoes, and fasten clothing. Instructors work with their behavior and their speech development. Children come to the institute with a variety of disabilities—cerebral palsy, seizure disorders, autism, hearing loss, cleft palate, and mental retardation—so the program for each child is individually designed.

In addition to the residential school for youths ages 6 to 22, there is a summer program which attracts additional students. The eight-week summer program combines classroom and life-skills training with fishing, swimming, camping, and nature activities. The institute also has a preschool program for children from two-and-a-half to six years of age and a parent-infant program to help family members learn techniques to use in the daily care of children with learning delays and handicaps. The institute is housed in 44 buildings on a 40-acre site just west of WSU. Last year the institute served 87 students from 26 states in its residential school, 343 area families in day programs, and 2,186 persons, mostly age 55 and over, in an audiology program.

A MEDICAL MECCA

Looking at the diplomas hanging on doctors' walls

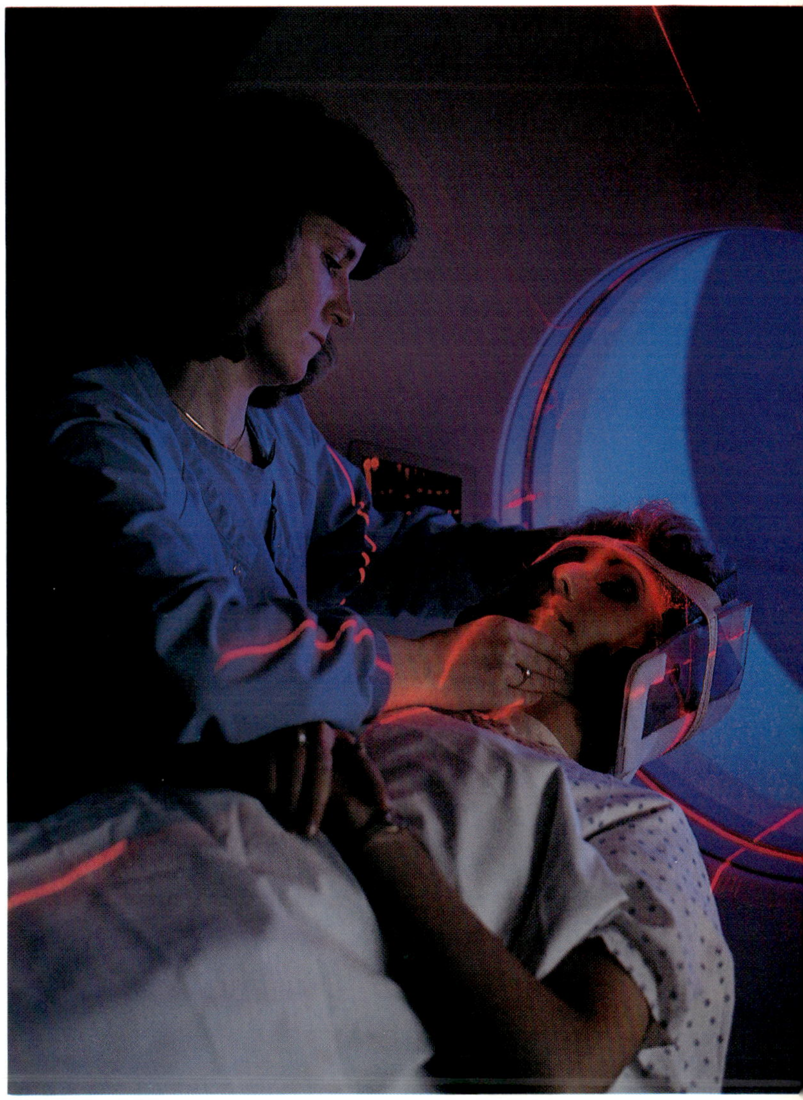

Bethany Medical Center offers the latest in technology. Pictured here is the CT 9800 computerized axial tomography whole body scanner. With this, physicians are able to quickly perform studies of the head and body tissued with unprecedented detail and accuracy. Courtesy, Bethany Medical Center/Marc Carver

in the greater Kansas City area as well as throughout the state, one would discover that a large percentage of them graduated from or did their internship or residency at the KU School of Medicine, one of the premier teaching hospitals in the Midwest. The KU Medical Center campus is located in Kansas City, Kansas, and the clinical branch is located in Wichita. Enrolled are more than 730 medical students and approximately 615 residents and fellows. Students seeking a degree in nursing number 236 and in allied health fields, 316. In addition there are nearly 500 graduate students. Allied health fields include cytotechnology, medical records administration, medical technology, and occupational, physical, and respiratory therapy. Last year KU Medical Center admitted 18,300 persons for inpatient care and treated 308,000 for outpatient services.

Bethany Medical Center and Providence-St. Margaret Health Center also are located in Wyandotte County. There are three major hospitals located in Johnson County—Shawnee Mission Medical Center, Humana Hospital, and Olathe Medical Center.

The state's other metropolitan area, Wichita, also provides major health services. In 1912 the Methodist church founded Wesley Hospital and Nurse Training Center. In 1986 Hospital Corporation of America bought Wesley and as a result the endowment arm of the hospital, created to sponsor specific projects and programs, severed its affiliation in order to retain its nonprofit status. Approximately $200 million from the sale was conveyed to the Wesley Foundation, making it one of the largest health care related foundations in the country. Today the foundation's scope has been broadened to back programs that enhance health care services and medical research throughout the state.

The Wesley Foundation, under the direction of a 69-member board of trustees, spends about $10 million annually. In 1987 the foundation awarded more than $220,000 through the Critically Underserved Partners Program, which helps rural Kansas in physician recruitment and retention. Recipients were Community Health Systems in Onaga, Ashland District Hospital, Lutheran Hospital Association in Hodgeman County, and the Jewell County United Methodist Parish. Since 1986 the Wichita Eye Foundation has received more than $450,000 for ophthalmic research and the development of an eye bank. Coffeyville Medical Center received a $5,000 grant for cholesterol screening and Victory in the Valley was awarded $65,000 for 1986 and 1987. This organization provides a support group and lodging for out-of-town cancer patients and their families who come to Wichita for treatment. In 1988 KU, K-State, and the KU Medical Center shared in a two-year cancer research grant of more than $1.8 million.

CITIES AND TOWNS

Wichita seems the appropriate place to begin a look at Kansas communities. It ranks as the state's largest city, with a population of 288,723, and each year it seems to take longer to cross from its east side to its west side. Boeing Military Airplanes in Wichita is the state's largest user of man power, with 24,000 employees. Beech, Cessna, and Piaggio aircraft companies also are located in Wichita and are major employers.

Older neighborhoods like Riverside still have a lot of appeal, with well-kept, tree-lined streets close to downtown, but residents will tell you the move is on to the northeast part of the city. That's where most of the newer houses have been built, where the best restaurants are located, and where new hotels are being placed.

Wichita is a mecca for shoppers in the western two-thirds of the state. Here they find necessities as well as luxuries in large, enclosed shopping malls and at discount houses.

Like Wichita, Johnson County and its myriad of communities have much to offer residents as well as visitors. No part of the state has changed as much as Johnson County in the past two decades. Less than 20 years ago Olathe, the county seat, had a population of just over 15,000. Now it ranks as the fifth-largest city in the state, with more than 52,180 residents. Driving south on Interstate 35, it's hard to tell where Merriam ends and Overland Park and Lenexa begin and when you reach the city limits of Olathe.

Over the last few years developers have turned the wide open spaces adjacent to College Boulevard in Overland Park into a city within the city, attracting new businesses as well as established firms which have either opened branch offices or moved entirely to this location. This growth has given impetus to the development of new hotels, like the Marriott and the Doubletree Inn, retail shops, restaurants, and housing.

The northern part of the county, where most of Johnson County's 21 cities are located, is usually referred to as Shawnee Mission. That's the name of the school district and the post office as well. The county is named after the Reverend Thomas Johnson, who founded the Shawnee Methodist Mission and Manual Training School. Between 200 and 300 Indian children studied there, labored on the adjacent 1,900-acre farm, and worked in the shops and mill. Three of the original buildings still stand in what is now the city of Fairway and are open to the public. Johnson is buried in the Indian cemetery nearby.

Also located in Shawnee Mission is one of the most affluent communities in America, Mission Hills. Mission Hills was the dream of J.C. Nichols, who also built Kansas City's Plaza shopping district and developed most of the property adjacent to Mission Hills on the Missouri side of State Line Road. Nichols envisioned a prestigious neighborhood of large, well-manicured lawns crowned by mansions designed in Italian, French, Spanish, and English styles. The first home was erected between 1912 and 1914. Adding to the splendor of the town of approximately 3,900 residents are outdoor sculptures, fountains, and urns. They enhance the park-like setting of the homes along streets which meander around the hills and spring-fed streams. The natural setting, with its abundance of trees and green space, makes Mission Hills a natural habitat for rabbits, squirrels, chipmunks, and red foxes.

Property values continue to escalate throughout Johnson County, where most homes sell for more than $100,000. In Mission Hills it is difficult to purchase any property for less than $300,000, and homes on larger lots are climbing toward the million-dollar mark.

There are many other communities in Kansas which have their own character, something special that makes them unique. Goessel is a good example. Settled in 1874 by German Mennonites who had emigrated from Russia, this small town still reflects that heritage. The Mennonites bought land in Harvey, Marion, and Reno counties. They brought with them only a few possessions, but their handmade chests contained one thing that changed the economy of Kansas: the seeds for Turkey Red wheat. The Mennonite farmers found the Kansas prairies similar to the steppes of Russia and the wheat adapted well to the soil.

Today Mennonites still worship at the large white Alexanderwohl church one mile north of Goessel. They have re-created the story of their immigrant ancestors at the Mennonite Heritage Museum. The Immigrant House is a facsimile of the long, barrack-like buildings used by the Santa Fe Railroad to house the Mennonites until they could build their own homes. According to museum treasurer Jan Schmidt, 40 families shared a house and each family was allowed 10 feet of space. Furniture and mannequins portray these living conditions. Chests and baskets brought from Russia are displayed along with family exhibits filled with personal heirlooms, photographs, and other records. In the Wheat Palace is the Wheat Straw Liberty Bell, made by the community to hang in the Smithsonian Institution during the Bicentennial. Made of Turkey Red wheat, the bell represents the Mennonite contribution to American agriculture. Antique tools, vehicles, farm machinery, and implements also are exhibited in the Wheat Palace.

With a population of more than a quarter of a million people, Wichita ranks as the state's largest city. Photo by Arni Katz

In southeast Kansas, coal, zinc, and lead put Pittsburg on the map. The best fried chicken in the world keeps it there. Who serves up the best chicken, cole slaw, potatoes, and onion rings? That depends upon whom you ask, but the two which seem to jockey for the number one position are Chicken Annie's and Chicken Mary's, located right next door to each other in almost identical buildings about five miles north of town.

Atchison, located on a high bluff above the Missouri River, has done an admirable job of preserving its wealth of Victorian homes. One of them is the birthplace of aviatrix Amelia Earhart. Because of its proximity to Wyandotte and Johnson counties, Atchison echoes with the sounds of city life unlike most of the state's small towns. It has the flavor of an old riverboat town.

Independence, about the same size as Atchison with a population of about 11,000, appears much more like a self-contained community.

Independence exudes small-town charm, the kind they portray in the movies. The town boasts a stable economy with a good education system, comprehensive hospital and health-care services, 37 churches, a high-rise apartment house for senior citizens, and even a park with a zoo. At Memorial Hall there are banquet facilities, five meeting rooms, two kitchens, and a 2,000-seat auditorium. The sports complex at the park includes a running track, swimming pool, 6 lighted tennis courts, 4 game fields, and 25 practice fields. The first night baseball game in America was played here in 1930. Once upon a time a baseball player by the name of Mickey Mantle played for the local farm club.

Independence is home to more than 170 retail firms, 5 financial institutions, and 5 major manufacturers employing more than 2,200 people. Five other companies employ an additional 600 persons. As in other Kansas towns, the citizens here are a friendly lot. If they know you're a stranger in town, they might even invite you home for dinner or at least to share a table at their favorite cafe.

FACING PAGE: This cyclist takes a break from a demanding ride. Photo by Keith Philpot

BELOW: The sun sets over a neighborhood church. Photo by Karen Mullen. Courtesy, Unicorn Stock Photos

Among the many festivals hosted in Lindsborg is the Hyllningsfest held biennially. Courtesy, Unicorn Stock Photos

4

THE CULTURAL TREASURY

The appreciation of music and art by the pioneers who settled Kansas set the stage more than a century ago for the cultural advantages which residents enjoy today. Early day recollections of life on the prairie demonstrate that fact. Joanna L. Stratton, referring to early day amusements in her book, *Pioneer Women*, states:

Literary societies emerged and provided weekly forums for debates, recitations, singing and dialogues within every growing community. Amateur theatrical groups, made up of the local talent, presented plays in the courthouse or the schoolroom, performing everything from lively informal skits to Shakespearean tragedies.

Today Kansas claims many cultural treasures from the fine arts to the performing arts. Many talented musical groups can be found throughout the state, and the most well-known among them is probably the Wichita Symphony Orchestra.

Founded in 1944, the Wichita Symphony boasts an 88-member orchestra which performs from September to May. According to general manager Mitchell Berman, the symphony offers a broad range of musical experiences. "We give between 50 and 80 performances annually," Berman said.

In addition to traditional concerts, the symphony performs chamber music recitals, pops concerts, and in-school programs. The orchestra tours the state and sponsors a youth orchestra and

Founded in 1944, the Wichita Symphony is an 88-member orchestra and has shared the stage with such internationally known artists as Mario Lanza, Beverly Sills, Itzhak Perlman, and Artur Rubenstein. Photo by Arni Katz

artist competitions. Michael Palmer is in his 13th season as conductor. Throughout its history, internationally known guest artists—Mario Lanza, Beverly Sills, Robert Merrill, Van Cliburn, Itzhak Perlman, and Artur Rubinstein, to name a few—have appeared with the symphony.

An annual May highlight of the symphony season is the Twilight Pops Concert, performed at the conclusion of the week-long Wichita River Festival. The program offers light classical and popular music and traditionally concludes with Tchaikovsky's *1812 Overture,* complete with cannons from Fort Riley and a fireworks display.

Most of the musicians only spend part of their time performing with the symphony. Approximately 75 to 80 percent of the musicians are former or present students and faculty members of Wichita State University. Five members also make up WSU's Lieurance Woodwind Quintet, which was established in 1946.

Each member of the quintet is a WSU professor. In 1985 the quintet toured Europe, performing 14 concerts in such cities as Salzburg and Venice. They have also appeared at New York's Carnegie Hall and in Washington, D.C., and tour Kansas as well as surrounding states with the Mid-America Arts Alliance. Members also give teaching as well as performing concerts, appearing in formal recitals, children's programs, lecture demonstrations for high school students, seminars and workshops for colleges, and radio and television broadcasts.

Like most community cultural groups, the symphony receives its financial support from a variety of sources. The Women's Symphony Society, with more than 450 members, has been a vital part of that support since 1946. Over the years the society has sponsored many types of fund-raising events, most recently the biennial Decorators' Showhouse.

A SWEDISH HERITAGE

Much of the cultural heritage of Kansas can be traced to Lindsborg, which was settled by Swedish immigrants from Varmland in 1869. Within a few years they founded Bethany College and began offering instruction in music and art.

The predominately Swedish community hosts many music and art celebrations throughout the year. The most widely known event is the eight-day Messiah Festival, which celebrated its 108th season in 1989. The 400-member Bethany Oratory Society, accompanied by the Bethany College Community Orchestra, presents Handel's *Messiah* on Palm Sunday and Easter and Bach's *Passion* on Good Friday. The performances are broadcast by WIBW radio station in Topeka for network satellite origination. During the Messiah Festival weekday concerts are offered by Bethany College choirs and instrumental ensembles. Guest artists as well as students give recitals. Dr. Elmer Copley, conductor and musical director for the society and Messiah Festival, retired in 1988 after 29 years of service.

Other festivals held in Lindsborg include Midsommers Dag, the St. Lucia Festival, and Hyllningsfest, which is held biennially. The October 1988 Hyllningsfest celebrated the Swedes who settled in the Smoky Valley area. Highlights of the three-day event included performances by the Lindsborg Adult Dancers, who keep Swedish folk dance traditions alive; the Lindsborg Swedish Folk Dancers and Fiddlers, a group of high school students that performs around the country and abroad; and elementary school students who demonstrated Swedish folk games set to music while dressed in colorful native costumes. There's always a parade and the 1988 honor band was from Hesston High School. The City of McPherson Pipe Band also marched in the parade. Always a sellout attraction is the Friday night smorgasbord, which is limited to 1,200 persons. In addition to more familiar dishes like Swedish meatballs, potato salad, and cole slaw, local cooks prepare 100 pounds of smoked salmon, 300 pounds of potato sausage, and 120

Home to many Swedish immigrants, Lindsborg offers arts and crafts to its local residents and tourists. Courtesy, Unicorn Stock Photos

pounds of sill (herring) salad as well as smoked tongue, brown beans, and a dessert known as Ost Kaka, which translates as cheesecake.

The St. Lucia Festival welcomes the Christmas season and includes carols by schools, community groups, and area musicians as well as folk dancing and an opportunity for visitors to sample Swedish holiday baked goods.

NATIONAL RECOGNITION

Another Lindsborg cultural legacy is that of the late Dr. Birger Sandzen, who had been an artist and a professor at Bethany College for 52 years. Sandzen used a variety of mediums—oils, watercolors, lithographs, and woodcuts—to interpret what he saw in the American West. His favorite subjects were willows and cottonwoods, ponds and riverbanks, pastures, pioneer houses, farms, rocks, and mountains. During his lifetime Sandzen produced more than 2,800 oil paintings, 400 watercolors, 328 prints, and many drawings. Much of his work can be seen in the Birger Sandzen Memorial Gallery at Bethany College. The gallery also displays other artists' work and often holds special exhibits and one-man shows. Sandzen art also hangs in New York's Metropolitan Museum of Art, the Chicago Art Institute, the British Museum, the Library of Congress, Kansas City's Nelson-Atkins Museum of Art, and private collections. But Lindsborg is not the only small town in Kansas whose culture has gained national recognition. Another is Independence.

The late William Inge, a Pulitzer prize-winning playwright, grew up here and attended Independence Community College. Inge is noted for his realistic psychological studies of ordinary people in small Midwestern towns. Anyone who has seen *Picnic, Bus Stop, Splendor in the Grass, The Dark at the Top of the Stairs,* or *Come Back, Little Sheba* will feel as though they have walked onto a stage set when they visit this southeast Kansas community and its surrounding towns. After Inge's death, Independence Community College inherited his manuscripts and personal library. The college sponsors the William Inge Festival and Conference, which is funded by grants from the Atlantic Richfield Foundation, Kansas Arts Commission, and Southwestern Bell Telephone Co. Playwrights like Garson Kanin (*Born Yesterday*) and Jerome Lawrence (*Inherit the Wind*) participate in the conference along with other members of the performing arts.

Local performers can show off their talents at the Topeka Civic Theatre. Photo by Rod Furgason. Courtesy, Unicorn Stock Photos

THEATER

Theatergoers throughout the state have a variety of productions from which to choose. Wichita provides good evidence of this. In addition to stage performances at Wichita State, the city also supports the Music Theater of Wichita, Wichita Community Theater, Empire House Restaurant and Theater, and Crown Uptown Dinner Theater. There's also the annual jazz festival.

Performers in Topeka also have several local outlets for their talents. There is a dinner theater, the Topeka Civic Theatre. There is also the Helen Hocker Performing Arts Center in Gage Park, and students at Washburn University perform with the University Players. Such musical groups as the Topeka Civic Symphony,

The Wichita Art Museum has a collection of American art, as well as a sculpture garden with more than 50 pieces of artwork. Photo by Perry Murphy. Courtesy, Unicorn Stock Photos

Chamber Music series, TOSCA Opera Club, and Topeka Jazz Workshop cater to a wide variety of tastes. Traveling shows appear at the Kansas Expocentre.

The theater department at the University of Kansas always offers an ambitious play season. They range from popular musicals like *Cabaret* to the children's classic, *Charlotte's Web,* and the Christmas opera, *Amahl and the Night Visitors.*

THE ARTS

The city of Lawrence, beneficiary of much of KU's cultural program, has a population of 56,500 with a large appetite for the arts. The historic city library building now houses the Lawrence Arts Center. Three thousand adults and children enrolled in 275 art classes and workshops at the center in 1987. More than 9,000 persons saw 21 exhibitions mounted in the center's Visual Arts Gallery, and 10,000 people attended more than 100 events in the Performance Hall. In addition to its normal classrooms, the center has a ceramics studio, photographic darkroom, and printmaking studio. The center also is home to the Seem-To-Be-Players, a children's theater company founded in 1973 by Ric Averill. The Seem-To-Be-

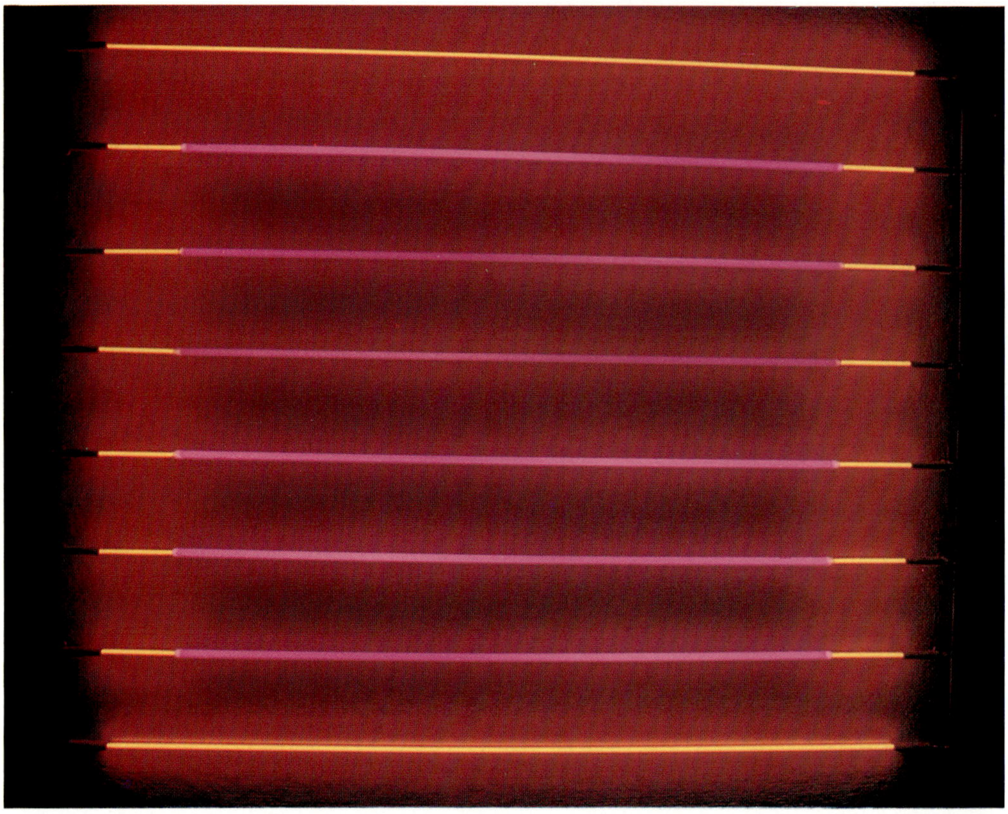

RIGHT: Although the Spencer Art Museum is noted for its medieval exhibits, it also contains contemporary Chinese and American art. Photo by Bob Barrett

BELOW: The Wichita Art Museum contains a wealthy collection of American Art that includes works from well-known artists as John Singleton Copley, Charles Russell, and Winslow Homer. Courtesy, Unicorn Stock Photos

Players used to perform in Lawrence every Saturday afternoon but now spend 8 to 10 weeks each year on tour, performing as well as conducting workshops in creative drama, storytelling, acting, improvisation, and children's theater. They appear four times annually in Lawrence.

Adjacent to KU is the Spencer Museum of Art, which owns one of the most comprehensive university art collections in the nation. Opened in 1977, the museum is noted for medieval art, European painting and sculpture, American painting and graphics, photography, Japanese Edo period painting, and contemporary Chinese painting. More than 25,000 objects are exhibited in 11 galleries. The museum is open year-round except on Mondays and holidays.

Overlooking the Spencer is the Museum of Natural History, which houses North American plants and animals in diorama format. Across the street is Spooner Hall, once the home of KU's art collection and now the residence of the Museum of Anthropology. Spooner, built in 1894, is the oldest remaining building on campus. Art lovers can whet their appetites elsewhere. In the rotunda of the state capitol in Topeka, murals by John Steuart Curry adorn the walls. The Mulvane Art Center on the Washburn campus houses paintings, prints, drawings, sculptures, and decorative art objects. The Mulvane also sponsors an art lecture series, tours to other museums, and children's art classes.

The Wichita Art Museum, located in the river park district, has a fine collection of American art, from the Colonial period to modern times. The Roland P. Murdock Collection includes oils by John Singleton Copley, Winslow Homer, William Bradford, Robert Henry, Charles Russell, and Horace Pippin. The Edwin A. Ulrich Museum of Art at Wichita State is adorned with a mural by Spanish artist Joan Miro. The outdoor sculpture garden has 50 pieces of artwork. The Wichita Art Association features traveling art exhibits, a children's theater, and junior gallery.

An unusual attraction in Oswego is the Ted Watts Sports Art Gallery. A nonprofit organization founded by Oswego businesspeople, the gallery contains more than 100 works of art by Watts. Illustrations by Watts hang in many other museums, including the Baseball Hall of Fame and Pro Football Hall of Fame.

During the summer many artistic attractions move outdoors. Sidewalk art shows, arts and crafts festivals in city parks, weekly bank concerts, and open-air theaters are popular throughout the state.

The Great Plains Chautauqua, a humanities tent show, takes place in Dodge City and Ottawa. It features scholars who present, in character, famous figures of American heritage. Public discussion follows.

Sandstone Amphitheater, located in Bonner Springs near Kansas City, books primarily one-night performances by rock, country, and western groups. Bonner Springs also is the location of the autumn Renaissance Festival. A benefit for the Kansas City Art Institute held over six weekends, the festival attracts thousands of spectators who come to mingle with costumed characters from the sixteenth century.

THE MEDIA

As many of the first settlers brought an appreciation for things cultural to their new home, so did they bring with them a curiosity about what was going on beyond their world. Between 1854 and 1936 more newspapers were published in Kansas than in any other state.

Among the leaders in print journalism is the Topeka Capital Journal. *Photo by Rod Furgason. Courtesy, Unicorn Stock Photos*

Even before the settlers arrived the Reverend Jotham Meeker, a missionary, brought the first printing press and type to the state, in 1833. He printed the first book in Kansas and published an Indian newspaper and many books in the Ottawa language. According to early records, the first newspaper was the *Leavenworth Herald*, founded in June 1854. In the pre-Civil War era, Kansas newspapers were political tools, espousing either freedom or slavery. Later the early newspapers found their way to other parts of America and Europe, and through vivid and often exaggerated descriptions enticed readers to come discover the joys of living in the West.

Many of the state's weekly and daily newspapers provided a training ground for budding politicos and journalists. One man in particular created a new approach to editorial writing which influenced not only the political and social views of Kansans but had an impact on newspaper readers throughout the United States. That man was William Allen White, editor/owner of the *Emporia Gazette* from 1895 until his death in 1944. White wrote editorials with a personal and dogmatic slant and minced no words when reporting on public figures and institutions.

When White wrote an editorial titled "What's the Matter with Kansas?" he took a swipe at the Populist party and William Jennings Bryan, which many historians believe was the first effective Republican propaganda and helped elect William McKinley to the presidency. In 1923 White won the Pulitzer prize for his editorial "To An Anxious Friend," which defended First Amendment speech and press rights. White has been called the most influential American editor of his day.

During the White era two newspaper dynasties came into being in Kansas: Harris Enterprises, Inc., and Stauffer Communications. Today both chains are still controlled by the respective families, with third and fourth generations still actively involved in the operations.

Oscar Stauffer worked as a $6-a-week reporter at the *Emporia Gazette* before becoming a publisher. Based in Topeka, Stauffer Communications owns the *Topeka Capital Journal*, WIBW-TV, and WIBW-AM and FM. Recently Stauffer bought newspapers in Tennessee and Florida. The chain also owns the *Independence* (Missouri) *Examiner* and the Kansas City Royals Radio Baseball Network. Stauffer formerly owned the *Kansas City Kansan* and newspapers in Arkansas City, Newton, and Peabody.

Ralph Harris bought the *Ottawa Herald* in 1907 and his two sons, John and Sidney, began buying other papers in the 1920s and 1930s. Today the Harris group includes eight newspapers in Kansas—the *Ottawa Herald, Olathe Daily News, Parsons Sun, Garden City Telegram, Hutchinson News, Salina Journal, Hays Daily News,* and *Chanute Tribune.* The chain's largest newspaper, the *Hutchinson News*, has a paid circulation of 41,674. Harris newspapers always have taken pride in their independent stance on issues and editorial policies. They cover day-to-day community events, from school board meetings to flower shows and high school sports, but never shy away from investigative reporting.

The state's broadest-based newspaper is the *Wichita Eagle-Beacon*, which has a weekday circulation of 124,054 and a Sunday circulation of 195,992. Founded in 1872 as two separate newspapers, the publications merged in 1960 and today the *Eagle-Beacon* is owned by Knight-Ridder. The paper is distributed in the western and southeastern parts of the state as well as in the Wichita area. Its publisher is Reed Ashe.

Today communications in Kansas go far beyond the printed word. The Kansas Association of Broadcasters has more than 150 member radio stations and more than 20 television stations. KCMO-AM radio in Fairway is the originating station for the Kansas City Chiefs' football games, which are broadcast to 23 Kansas towns. WIBW originates broadcast of the Kansas City Royals' baseball games to 33 stations.

From its simple pioneer beginnings, this territory called Kansas has matured and prospered, high stepping into the twenty-first century.

With more than 150 radio and 20 television stations, just a touch of a button brings Kansans news of the world. Photo by Arni Katz

Kansas is the first in production of wheat and ranks among the leaders nationwide in cash receipts from farm products. Photo by Keith Philpott

PART

II

KANSAS MEANS BUSINESS

By Ron Welch

For Kansas, wheat represents its economic strength. Photo by Bruce Mathews

5

GROWING STRONG

Visual reminders of the importance of agribusiness to the Kansas economy are virtually everywhere in the state. Massive grain elevators, the "skyscrapers of the plains," often are the largest structures in cities and towns. Farms—70,000 of them—dot the rural landscape. The head of wheat on Kansas' motor vehicle license plates is emblematic of the state's close ties to the land. Agribusiness is the state's single biggest industry.

Winter wheat comprises more than 35 percent of all products grown in Kansas, making it the number one cash crop. Farmers plant the grain in the fall and normally reap bumper harvests in June. In non-drought years, recent annual crops have averaged 300 million to 400 million bushels. Penalties for this abundance, however, have been severe. Low prices have limited the value of crops to around $750 million annually.

The rising star on the Kansas agribusiness scene is the beef industry. In 1988 it contributed $6 billion to $8 billion, directly and indirectly, to the state's economy. Kansas is one of the nation's largest cattle feeders and America's leading packer of red meat.

The average number of cattle slaughtered in the state annually has more than doubled the 1980 figure. Nearly 6.3 million of the animals were processed at Kansas packing plants in 1988, accounting for 18 percent of the United States total.

Southwest Kansas, particularly, is benefiting from the growth of the beef packing industry. Enough cattle are processed daily in Finney County (population 30,000) to feed a city of one million for an entire month. Garden City, the Finney County seat, has seen its population swell by nearly 30 percent since 1980. The increase parallels the opening of several major meat processors in the area.

FACING PAGE, TOP: This custom wheat-cutting crew member is hard at work. Photo by Jeff Hetler. Courtesy, Unicorn Stock Photos

FACING PAGE, BOTTOM: The raising of cattle and hogs is a chief source of agricultural income in Kansas. Photo by Arni Katz

IBP, Inc., the world's largest beef packer, processes thousands of animals daily in Emporia and employs more than 2,600 persons at its plant seven miles west of Garden City. Another 1,000 people work at the Swift facility east of Garden City. Dodge City and Liberal also are enjoying a "beef boom" as Excel, HyPlains, and National operate large plants in those communities.

Kansans have a number of reasons to be optimistic about the growth of the cattle feeding and slaughtering industries in the state. One is the improving image of red meat.

Per capita consumption of beef dropped significantly in the United States during the last decade. Much of the decline could be attributed to negative reports on the product from various health organizations. Among other things, it "increases blood cholesterol levels," they said. Unfortunately for the industry, data supporting these findings was based on research done more than 20 years ago. Modern beef is leaner and trimmer than ever before and provides a large amount of nutrients for a small number of calories. Cholesterol also has been reduced.

According to the American Heart Association, today's beef is "hard to beat . . . as an excellent source of proteins, vitamins and minerals, including iron." Leaner beef is the result of changes that have been implemented in the marketing chain, from producers to retailers. More cattle are crossbred for a better product. Also, the amount of time animals are grain fed has been shortened.

Nationally, radio, television, newspaper, and magazine ads are telling Americans that beef is "Real Food For Real People." The advertising campaign's target market is people in the 25-54 age bracket, considered "light users" by the beef industry because they consume red meat less than six times in a two-week period. A more localized marketing program features Kansas City Royals' infielder George Brett urging everyone to "Eat Like An All Star."

Much of the funding for these promotions comes from a $1-per-head checkoff that mandates that one dollar be collected each time an animal is sold. More than $9 million was raised through this procedure in Kansas in 1988.

Some companies, like Excel, are branching into specialty products. Its "branded beef," for example, is being marketed in vacuum-packed, leak-proof packages like those used by poultry and pork sellers. Other Kansas red meat packers are contemplating moves into the consumer-ready product line.

The "trickle-down" effects of stepped-up beef processing have been dramatic. IBP opened a blue-chrome tannery in 1984 and already it is the third-largest domestic tannery in the world. A new container shipping company in Garden City primarily ships hides. Local retailers have had to expand.

Anthony's, a store in downtown Garden City, is a good example of that expansion. Business has increased so much over the past 10 years that the retailer has moved into a building three times the size of its original 16,200-square-foot structure. Manager Everett Stewart says, "The packing houses have brought the trucking industry, box factories, and more people. And it has changed our lives. It has been tremendous."

FEEDLOTS SUPPLY MEAT PACKERS

Kansas has become the hub of the cattle feeding industry says Rich McKee, executive secretary of the Kansas Livestock Association's feedlot division.

"Only Texas and Nebraska have more animals in their yards than we do," he notes, "and we are continually jockeying with Nebraska for the runner-up slot."

He adds that five major packers alone slaughter almost 25,000 cattle a day. They rely heavily on the state's 100-plus commercial feedlots for much of their supply.

"We get cattle from every state and Mexico," McKee says. "Producers go where the cheapest feed and the best markets are and, for many of them, that's here."

The first commercial Kansas feedlot was started by Earl Brookover near Garden City in the 1950s. In 1971 the state ranked sixth nationally in fed cattle marketed. Growth has been rapid.

Capacity at Kansas feedlots varies from 1,000 to 2,000 head at smaller operations to 100,000 at the giant Caprock facility near Leoti. Some 4.7 percent of the feedlots have a capacity of 8,000 head or greater.

Cattle spend anywhere from 95 to 125 days in a Kansas feedlot depending on their incoming weight and rate of weight gain. While there, they are fed a scientifically formulated ration scrutinized regularly by a professional nutritionist. Each batch of feed is individually mixed and loaded. Bunks are filled at least twice a day.

Most feedlots use a four-step ration system. The cattle are started on a relatively low-energy diet after being unloaded from trucks. The idea is to give them something they like to eat, such as hay, on arrival. Then, as quickly as possible, they're switched to an extremely high-energy diet.

All cattle are supervised from receiving to market and are vaccinated and checked as they arrive. Pen riders continually work their way through the herds looking for livestock that might be ill so that veterinarians may treat them. Weekly and bimonthly reports on the cattle are sent to their owners. When the animals are

Breeding, feeding for the market, and dairying are all included in the livestock industry. Photo by John Elk III

ready for market, show lists are sent to packers.

The top five counties in number of fed cattle marketed are Finney, Scott, Ford, Wichita, and Haskell, all in the southwest corner of the state. There are a number of reasons for this concentration. Ample supplies of grain and roughage are available in the area at a price that is cost effective. The climate is moderate. There are fewer hot days than in areas farther south and a lesser number of cold days than in states to the north. A sparse rainfall means a limited number of "mud days," thus minimizing the chance that the cattle will contract diseases associated with wet weather.

"Then, of course, there's the proximity of the feedlots to the packers," emphasizes McKee. "Shorter trips to the plants mean less stress on the livestock and lower costs of shippers and receivers."

McKee claims the future is bright for the state's feedlot industry, and for Kansas beef in general.

"We've been successful in communicating to the legislature and to other regulators that ours is a mobile industry that deals in a transient product and shouldn't be taken for granted," he says. "It's also a highly competitive business and cattlemen must get a return for their investment. If our feedlots get out of line in cost comparisons with other states, the cattle will be shipped elsewhere.

"Our beef also is recognized worldwide for its quality," he continues. "Many restaurants from coast to coast now specify on their menus that the steaks they offer come from Kansas. What they're attempting to convey to their customers is that the product they're serving isn't just any beef, it's the best!"

HOGS, SHEEP, AND LAMBS

More than one million hogs are slaughtered in Kansas annually and that figure isn't expected to change much in the near future. Sheep and lamb kills, however, have escalated dramatically.

Only 6,000 sheep and lambs were processed in the state during 1984. By 1988 that figure had reached 436,000 and Kansas' slaughter ranking for the animals had jumped from 24th in the nation to 5th.

"Most of that growth is attributable to one packing plant operated by the Monfort Company in Harper," says Cliff Spaeth, a Kansas State University sheep specialist. "It's one of only 12 in the United States that slaughters in excess of 100,000 head a year."

Spaeth says most of the processed meat is sold on the East Coast and there isn't much local demand for the product. He expects a 10 to 20 percent growth in the next few years and also a slight increase in the number of feedlots supplying the livestock.

"There are now three major feedlots in the Harper vicinity capable of maintaining 60,000 to 70,000 sheep and lambs," he notes. "Any expansions will be moderate in size."

AMERICA'S BREADBASKET

More wheat is produced in Kansas than in any other state. Kansas is also number one in wheat flour milling capacity and wheat flour milled.

After some "lean" years during the first half of the 1980s, Kansas' 46,000 wheat farmers have good reason to be optimistic that the demand for their product will

ABOVE: A worker checks the top of a grain storage bin. The silos are usually the tallest structures in town and have earned the nickname "skyscrapers of the plain." Photo by Jeff Hetler. Courtesy, Unicorn Stock Photos

RIGHT: A small sample of wheat is collected to check for moisture content. Photo by Jeff Hetler. Courtesy, Unicorn Stock Photos

A combine harvests hard red winter wheat in Kiowa County. Photo by Keith Philpot

increase. America's per capita annual consumption of wheat food products rose three pounds in 1988 to 128 pounds. Exports, particularly to the Soviet Union and China, have sharply depleted reserves in grain elevators, terminals, and other storage facilities.

Sharon Davis, nutritionist for the Kansas Wheat Commission, points out that wheat consumption dropped in the 1970s when consumers avoided breads and the starch they contain, thinking they were major contributors to weight gain.

"With the aid of various health organizations we've been able to convince people that eating more complex carbohydrates is good for them," she says. "New products in the baking industry also have increased the demand for wheat.

"For example, it wasn't long ago that most supermarkets had a row of prepackaged buns, breads, rolls, and little else in the baked goods line," she continues. "Now they try to outdo one another for freshness and variety of their products. Bakeries often are one of the most important and profitable sections of stores."

Most of the wheat grown in Kansas is of the hard red winter class. Because it contains relatively high amounts of gluten-forming protein, it almost always is used in the making of bread. Gluten is a tenacious, elastic protein substance that gives cohesiveness to dough.

Kansas farmers usually transport their harvested wheat to one of the more than 900 local grain elevators scattered across the state. These elevators have a storage capacity of more than 913 million bushels and give Kansas a third-place ranking nationally in that category.

Wheat leaving grain elevators is shipped to flour mills or exported. More than two-thirds of all Kansas production leaves the country, primarily through Gulf Coast terminals. Some mills also double as exporters, bagging flour and wheat for shipment overseas. The State of Kansas is the leading flour exporter in the U.S.

FACING PAGE: The sun sets but the work continues. Photo by Les Van. Courtesy, Unicorn Stock Photos

MANHATTAN, KANSAS

Manhattan, Kansas, is the focal point of the United States and the world for cereal grain research and baking technology. The city is home to Kansas State University's milling and grain science departments, the U.S. Department of Agriculture's grain marketing research lab, the Wheat Quality Council, and the one-of-a-kind American Institute of Baking (AIB).

The AIB, founded in 1919, moved to Manhattan from Chicago in 1977. It is a nonprofit organization funded by more than 800 food processing companies. Throughout its history it has played a major role in training individuals and transferring baking and bakery technology throughout the world.

"We're problem solvers as well as educators," says John Cannon, AIB communications coordinator. "We've developed formula and process for white pan bread in the People's Republic of China, demonstrated a novel method for making bread with low-cost ingredients in Sri Lanka, developed thick- and thin-crust style pizzas for use in a Venezuelan fast-food restaurant chain, experimented with improving the buns of a well-known American hamburger chain, even came up with a better breading for a major national fried chicken outlet."

Another product developed at the AIB, in cooperation with the Kansas Restaurant Association, Kansas Wheat Commission, Kansas Honey Producers, Kansas State Board of Agriculture, and Kansas mix-manufacturer CPI Corporation, is "SunnyWheat" bread. According to Sharon Davis, nutritionist for the Kansas Wheat Commission, it's "a specialty bread mix chock full of Kansas agricultural goodness."

The bread is a blend of Kansas flour, cracked wheat, rolled oats, sunflower seeds, honey, soybean oil, milk, and salt. Because it is such a flavorful, hearty mixture of grains, the bread was offered at Bloomingdale's department stores in New York as part of a Kansas specialty foods promotion.

SunnyWheat is now on the shelves of many Kansas supermarkets and is proudly served at a number of the state's finest restaurants. It is hoped that the bread will give Kansas a truly nationally known specialty food item similar in popularity to San Francisco's sourdough bread.

"We're proud of the role AIB had in the development of SunnyWheat," Cannon says, "and of the importance our institute plays in the food industry throughout the world. We export knowledge . . . 30 percent of all of our students are from foreign countries . . . and hope that what they learn here will not only benefit them, but also prove profitable for the American grain industry by increasing the demand for its products."

FINDING THEIR NICHE

"Great Plains Red" specialty wheat is a result of varietal selection of the grain in western Kansas. It averages 2.5 percent higher in protein content and has better milling and baking characteristics than hard red winter wheat. Consequently, it commands a premium in the marketplace some 20 percent per bushel above other wheats.

As president and general manager of the WaKeeney-based Great Plains Red, Inc., Mark Karlin signs up farmers to grow the specialty wheat and makes sure that their production methods conform to his specifications.

"They must agree to keep our variety separate from other wheat and store it away from insects," he says. "It is essential that special agronomic practices be

FACING PAGE: The final product after a good harvest: some of the finest specialty breads available. Photo by James Jackson. Courtesy, Tony Stone Worldwide

followed to preserve the integrity of Great Plains Red."

Karlin and his group of investors say theirs is one of the first attempts in recent years to put farmers on a strict production schedule. The goal is to provide the tools for a farmer to become a manufacturer of a better product and to be rewarded for that extra effort.

"Because margins are so tight none of us is a millionaire yet," he emphasizes, "but Great Plains Red has enormous potential. The Cargill Company buys all we can produce for use in its white pan and specialty bread. We've filled a niche for them with something they can't purchase elsewhere and they've made our entrepreneurial endeavors worthwhile.

"Other companies have needs that are going unfulfilled," Karlin concludes. "We will continue to be aggressive in seeking them out. Although we've found a niche with Cargill we know that complacency is the answer to very little. Increased enrollment by farmers in our Great Plains Red program will necessitate new markets for their wheat."

Loren Swenson and Mak McGaughey also are farmers who've opted to become entrepreneurs. They've developed and are successfully marketing the LorMak brand of stone-ground whole wheat flour, cracked wheat cereal, whole wheat biscuit mix, and whole wheat and buttermilk pancake and waffle mix.

"My wife started gardening organically," recalls Swenson. "Having been brought up in a chemical world it was a process completely foreign to me. However I tried it with a small amount of wheat and liked the results."

Swenson was at a loss as to what to do with the organically grown wheat other than to blend it with other grain for delivery to a Concordia elevator.

"A local food store manager suggested I grind it up and he'd sell it," Swenson adds. "It went over well with his customers and now we're selling it in more than 150 stores."

LorMak needed only 150 bushels of wheat to meet consumer demand during 1985, the first year of the venture. That jumped to 2,000 bushels the second year and doubled again to 4,000 bushels in 1988.

Swenson says the process LorMak employs for grinding is a simple one. Two electrically operated granite stones crush the wheat kernels between them. Since the wheat is ground at a lower temperature than at most mills, 85 percent of the B-complex vitamins are preserved.

Marketing has been done "by knocking on doors." Product testing is at the grass-roots level.

"We get our friends and neighbors to eat our experiments," Swenson chuckles. "We also try everything out on ourselves. It's not scientific but it works."

Packaging has improved from plastic bags placed inside a paper sack with a label on it to professional containers purchased from Midco Plastics of Enterprise, Kansas.

Current employees include the Swenson and McGaughey families and wives and kids of neighbors.

Three other products may soon be added to the LorMak lineup. One is a spice flour breading for use on fish, wild game, and pork chops.

"We are excited about LorMak and its potential," says Swenson. "It gives us control over what we grow from the field to the stores and guarantees us a more steady income."

A freight train rumbles through Lenexa. Photo by Keith Philpott

6

"AMERICA'S CROSSROADS"

Horace Greeley, a famous nineteenth-century New York journalist, once advised his countrymen, "Go west, young man, go west."

Since then, Americans have done just that. The center of the U.S. population continues to move westward and southerly each year, inching its way toward Kansas.

Geographically, Kansas is at the center of the 48 contiguous United States. A monument near the north-central community of Lebanon marks the spot.

This ideal location, at America, center stage, has proven attractive to many companies serving national or regional markets. By being at the heart of their distribution systems most have reduced their shipping costs, making it easier for them to generate profits.

Kansas has been at the focal point of America's transportation network since the Santa Fe, Chisholm, and Oregon trails traversed portions of the state. Over them traveled people, freight, and livestock. Their replacements, the interstates and primary highways, do the same things at a much more expeditious rate.

OVERVIEW

Kansas has the fifth-largest public roads system in the country. Its major interstates are I-70, which crisscrosses the state between Missouri on its eastern border and Colorado to the west, and I-35 and I-135, which provide access north and south. More than 8,000 miles of primary highways complement the interstate system.

All 960 populated Kansas communities are served by the trucking industry. A total of 287 of them, or 29.9 percent, depend entirely on the motor carriers for the surface transportation of intercity freight. Nearly 650,000 trucks operate in the state.

STRICK
Lease
AMERICAN

More than 11,500 of them are common carriers; another 5,200 are contract carriers.

Kansas also ranks sixth among the 50 states in total trackage for Class I rail carriers. Approximately 4 percent of all United States railroad miles are within the confines of Kansas—slightly more than 6,400 miles. The trackage total comprises 3,490 miles of main lines and 2,890 miles of branch lines. Freight service to 110 communities is provided by five Class I railroads and nine Class III companies.

Amtrak's rail passenger system operates daily runs through Kansas on its Chicago to Los Angeles and return route. Dodge City, Emporia, Garden City, Hutchinson, Lawrence, Newton, and Topeka are the Kansas cities it serves. And most major Kansas communities have bus passenger service; the Greyhound Corporation is the main provider.

FACING PAGE: Approximately 650,000 trucks make use of some 8,000 miles of highways in the state. Courtesy, Unicorn Stock Photos

Aviation has been one of the cornerstones of the state's economy, and emphasis has been placed on maintaining a well-developed airport system. The Federal Aviation Administration has approved operations at 384 airports and landing strips in Kansas, making the state the 12th-best in the nation in terms of air travel.

ABOVE: This Amtrak train services seven cities in the state on its Chicago-to-Los Angeles route. Photo by Martin R. Jones. Courtesy, Unicorn Stock Photos

Wichita Mid-Continent Airport is the largest of 149 airfields open for public use. (Approximately two-thirds of these airports have paved runways.) Nine major airlines, and commuter operations, serve Mid-Continent. Besides Wichita, other cities including Topeka, Salina, Hays, and Dodge City have regularly scheduled air passenger service.

Contrary to popular belief, Kansas isn't a totally landlocked state. The Missouri River forms 122 miles of the state's border, from the Nebraska state line to Kansas City. Eighteen port terminals are scattered from White Cloud south. The major ones are at Atchison, Leavenworth, and Kansas City.

During World War II Leavenworth had an active shipbuilder, Missouri Valley Steel, Inc., that manufactured hundreds of landing craft for military use plus tugboats and barges. The completed vessels were floated down river to the Mississippi, then on to New Orleans. The company constructed tugs and barges for civilian use until a few years ago.

The bulk of shipments from Kansas ports are foodstuffs, fertilizers, and machinery. Port usage was down in 1988 because of drought conditions that led to less grain being shipped. The Missouri River shipping season is between eight and nine months long depending on winter conditions.

HIGHWAYS

The Kansas Department of Transportation is responsible for maintaining the roads and bridges of the state highway system. Its emphasis has been on preservation and modernization of existing highways because revenues have not kept pace with inflation, a problem familiar to most states.

The latest study of vehicle miles traveled in Kansas discloses that they are up 2.5 billion over the 1980 figure. Yet motor fuel tax receipts are only $33 million

Tax-free revenues from tolls are used to maintain and operate state roads and highways. Courtesy, Unicorn Stock Photos

above those of 1980. State motor fuel tax rates, per gallon, were raised in 1989 to 15 cents for gasoline and gasohol, 17 cents for diesel, and 14 cents for liquid propane. Only nine states have lower rates.

Taxes on motor fuel provide funding for 30.4 percent of state highway expenditures. The following sources pay for the remainder of the costs: federal funds, 31.1 percent; registration fees, 22.5 percent; sales tax transfer, 12.3 percent; and other sources, 3.7 percent.

In April 1989 the Kansas Legislature approved a $2.6-billion, 8-year highway program to provide new and improved roadways.

A HIGHWAY SUCCESS STORY

In the 1950s bonds were sold in Kansas to build a turnpike from Kansas City to South Haven. The roadway was constructed in a 22-month period and opened to traffic on October 25, 1956.

Today's Kansas Turnpike is nearly 250 miles long and provides a connecting link for the eastern terminal, near Kansas City at Bonner Springs, with Interstate 35 at the Oklahoma border. It passes through such major cities as Lawrence, Topeka, Emporia, El Dorado, and Wichita.

Funds for the turnpike's maintenance and operation are provided solely by tolls and other revenue generated by its users. No tax monies of the people of the state of Kansas are involved.

In accordance with the Surface Transportation and Uniform Relocation Assistance Act of 1987, the speed limit was raised to 65 mph on many of America's rural interstate highways. Interstate 35 and 70 designated sections of the Kansas Turnpike were quickly changed from the former 55 mph maximum speed limit to 65 mph. Later the 50-mile stretch of turnpike from Emporia to Topeka was designated Interstate 335, which also made it eligible for the increased 65 mph limit.

Eighteen toll plazas are strategically placed along the turnpike route. There are six service areas, in Lawrence, Topeka, Emporia, Matfield Green, Towanda, and Belle Plaine. Service stations at them are leased to Coastal Mart (formerly Derby), which dispenses fuel at prices competitive with those in cities through which the turnpike operates. Hardee's is the fast-food provider at five of the service areas while McDonald's has the Emporia franchise.

The number of vehicles using the Kansas Turnpike in 1988 was up 7.66 percent from the previous year, a total of 17,569,053 vehicles. Of that amount, 14,711,165, or 83.73 percent, were passenger cars and the rest were commercial vehicles. All vehicles combined were driven 784,370,639 miles, a 8.7 percent increase over the miles logged on the turnpike the previous year.

The average revenue to the turnpike per trip for commercial vehicles was $4.88. For passenger cars it was $1.41. Approximately one-third of the money allocated by the Kansas Turnpike Authority is for maintenance. The 1988 figure was slightly over $5.5 million.

The turnpike has a good safety record that can be attributed to, among other things, concentrated Highway Patrol enforcement and the installation of a concrete median barrier from Kansas City to Topeka which has eliminated head-on collisions. Additionally, an improved new guardrail system around bridge piers and other fixed objects has significantly reduced the severity of many accidents.

The Kansas Turnpike Authority also maintains the Kansas City Expressway. This important metropolitan toll artery was used by nearly 2.73 million vehicles in 1988.

KANSAS' TRUCKING INDUSTRY

Trucking is big business in Kansas. The more than 100,000 individuals employed in the industry receive an annual payroll in excess of $1.7 billion.

Motor carriers transport virtually 100 percent of Kansas-grown fresh fruits and vegetables to the nation's principal markets. They also carry 100 percent of livestock, nearly all poultry and eggs, and more than 90 percent of fresh and frozen meat destined for consumers. In all, nearly 90 percent of the state's agricultural products are

LEFT: Almost 90 percent of the state's agricultural products are hauled from farms to initial markets by trucks. Photo by Aneal Vohra. Courtesy, Unicorn Stock Photos

BELOW: More than 100,000 employees are employed in the trucking industry. Photo by Aneal Vohra. Courtesy, Unicorn Stock Photos

This mechanic sees to it that the trucks are well maintained to service the public. Photo by Bob Barrett

hauled from farms to initial markets by trucks.

No other business affects our daily lives more directly than the motor carrier industry. The clothes we wear, food we eat, cars we drive, and things we use in making a living come to us all or part of the way in a truck. The industry's slogan—"If You've Got It—A Truck Brought It"—sums up the dependency of Kansas, and the nation, on this form of highway transportation.

Motor carriers operating in and through the state are permitted a maximum gross weight of 80,000 pounds on the interstate highway system. The corresponding maximum gross weight on the state highway system is 85,000 pounds.

The maximum total length for a single truck is 42.5 feet. For a semitrailer it's 65 feet. "Doubles" (two shortened trailers pulled by a single tractor) are allowed on some Kansas roadways and the Kansas Turnpike permits triple trailers.

Of the thousands of truck lines operating in and through Kansas, more than 1,550 of them belong to the Kansas Motor Carriers Association. Since 1936 this group has helped the highway transportation industry improve its service to the public and achieve its present stature.

A number of Kansas-based trucking companies are well-known in the transportation industry. American Carriers, in Overland Park, is a general commodities carrier. The Becker Corporation, of El Dorado, transports gas, asphalt, and oil in its tankers. Branson Truck Lines, based in Lyons, is one of the largest employers in Rice County. It hauls livestock in its fleet of 29 trucks.

Ideal Truck Lines has enjoyed success as a general commodities carrier operating from the northwestern Kansas community of Norton. Tollie Freightways is an irregular route carrier based in Kansas City.

One of Kansas' largest trucking firms is Yellow Freight System, Inc., which provides less-than-truckload (LTL) shipments of general commodities to 50 states, Puerto Rico, and the Canadian provinces of Alberta, Manitoba, and Quebec. Headquartered in Overland Park, the company also has operations in the Canadian provinces of British Columbia and Ontario in conjunction with subsidiaries.

Company founder A.J. Harrell began Yellow Cab Transit Co. in Oklahoma City in 1924, but later shortened the name to Yellow Transit Co. In those early years his "system" consisted of two trucks delivering goods between Tulsa and Oklahoma City, a distance of about 100 miles.

The company's revenues first exceeded $1 million annually in 1938. George E. Powell, the current chairman of the board and chief executive officer, and a group of his associates acquired Yellow in 1952. Under his direction the firm's annual revenues passed the $100 million mark for the first time in 1966, and exceeded $600 million in 1977.

Yellow Freight System, Inc., has grown rapidly in the 1980s. A hub-and-spoke freight flow system implemented in 1981 has provided the base for a rapid increase in the company's terminal network. Today's system is an intricate network of 600-plus terminals and 24 hubs serving more than 30,000 U.S. and Canadian communities as well as importers and exporters worldwide.

Yellow Freight System, Inc., is now a wholly owned subsidiary of its holding company, Yellow Freight System, Inc. of Delaware, under a tax-free reorganization. The company generates more than $1.5 billion in revenues annually.

THE HORATIO ALGER OF KANSAS COMMUTER AVIATION

Gary Adamson's start in the world of commercial aviation wasn't in the most glamorous of jobs. With one single-engine Cessna 206 he began delivering bodies to funeral operators in 1965.

Adamson's company, Aviation Services, Inc. (ASI), was the forerunner of successful Air Midwest. It experienced financial difficulties early on and Adamson expanded its scope of operations to include air ambulance services. Later he began to transport freight and even offered flying lessons and carried skydivers to keep his business afloat.

In 1967 Central Airlines announced it would discontinue flights on its Wichita-Salina route. ASI, with Adamson as the only pilot, began making twice daily round-trips between the two Kansas cities. Although the route proved unprofitable, a second route, from Wichita to Springfield, Missouri, was added. Adamson reasoned that if his aircraft was used for more hours per day it would help his profit picture.

Later that year ASI hired a second pilot and acquired a certificate for transporting U.S. mail. In October 1968 the carrier began to provide air service in Dodge City, replacing Frontier Airlines under one of the first route replacement programs authorized by the Civil Aeronautics Board. ASI carried approximately 5,000 passengers that year and expanded the number of aircraft it flew to five.

On March 15, 1969, ASI's board of directors voted to change the name of the company to Air Midwest. The new designation was designed to emphasize the company's new role as a scheduled air carrier.

During the early 1970s Air Midwest continued to add more cities to its routes. By May 1972 it was shuttling passengers between seven Kansas communities, three Colorado cities, and Kansas City.

In 1975 the airline filed for certification as a regional air carrier and was awarded a Certificate of Public Convenience and Necessity as the nation's first "regional" feeder air carrier. At the time only Ozark Airlines was operating with a similar certificate.

Other milestones in Air Midwest's history occurred in 1977, when the company began operating turboprop aircraft, and 1983, when *Air Transport World* magazine named it the Regional/Commuter Airline of the Year for 1982.

Air Midwest is presently affiliated with two major air carriers, Braniff Airlines and Trans World Airlines, in an air express network. Trans World Express, with St. Louis as its hub, provides scheduled air service to communities in Iowa, Missouri, Minnesota, Arkansas, Illinois, Tennessee, Kentucky, Alabama, and Indiana. Braniff Express, with Kansas City as its hub, serves Kansas, Colorado, Oklahoma, Arkansas, Iowa, Wisconsin, Illinois, Missouri, and Nebraska. The express system schedules approximately 400 flights on weekdays.

Air Midwest, headquartered in Wichita, employs 1,000 persons and flies nearly 50 aircraft. They range from 17-passenger Fairchild Metro IIs to Embraer Brasilias

The multimillion-dollar air terminal at Topeka's Forbes Field speaks for the success the facility has enjoyed in recent years. Photo by Bob Barrett

and Saab 340s with capacities of up to 30 persons.

Air Midwest transported more than one million passengers, for the first time, in 1987. The carrier's gross revenue amounted to $68 million that year.

KANSAS' AIRPORT SYSTEM

Scheduled air passenger service is offered at 12 Kansas airports. Airfields are located in Wichita, Topeka, Manhattan, Salina, Hays, Garden City, Liberal, Dodge City, Great Bend, Hutchinson, and near Parsons. Additionally, many eastern Kansans avail themselves of the extensive airline services offered at Kansas City International Airport.

The highest enplanement activity in the state occurs at Wichita Mid-Continent Airport. The field is served by 10 airlines: Air Midwest (Braniff Express), American, America West, Braniff, Continental, Delta, Northwest, TWA, United, and USAir.

These commercial airlines fly an average of 55 departures per day, with nonstop service to nine hubs. The top 10 destinations for Mid-Continent's more than one million passengers annually are Denver, Dallas/Fort Worth, Chicago, Los Angeles, Phoenix, Houston, Las Vegas, Seattle, New York, and St. Louis.

Mid-Continent has the distinction of being the only Kansas site of an automated flight service station, operated by the Federal Aviation Administration. Further, the airport is one of a handful of sites for the FAA's pilot program for a microwave landing system. In 1986 Mid-Continent also was the first airport in the nation to completely automate its entire range of administrative and operating activities.

Wichita's major airport is classified as a medium-hub commercial service airport in the National Plan of Integrated Airport Systems. It has three runways that vary in length from 6,301 feet to 10,300 feet.

Rounding out the Kansas aviation infrastructure at Mid-Continent and other airports are a number of air cargo companies. Direct cargo service is offered from Wichita to Los Angeles, New York City, Denver, Dallas/Fort Worth, Kansas City, St. Louis, and other important cities by such air cargo industry leaders as Airborne Freight Corp., Emery Air Freight, Federal Express Corp., and United Parcel Service.

Topeka's Forbes Field boasts a new multimillion-dollar air terminal, and the Metropolitan Topeka Airport Authority is actively seeking a major commercial air passenger carrier to serve it. In the meantime, several commuter airlines fly in and out of the facility.

Forbes Field and the Salina Municipal Airport are former U.S. Air Force installations that were ordered to close in the 1970s. Both have prospered since civilian businesses took over and renovated abandoned buildings and constructed new ones. The airfields have also been actively used as temporary training bases for military aviators and civilian aircrews, who like the advantages of long runways and uncongested air space for practicing maneuvers.

RAILROADS

The importance of railroading in Kansas, from the mid-1800s to the twentieth century, cannot be overemphasized. Trains were the lifeblood of prairie communities. Cities sprung up overnight on speculation that rail lines would be built through them. Achilles, Ash Valley, Cash City, Mingo, Santa Fe, Sheridan, and others came and died when the railroads bypassed or abandoned them.

Railroad ventures were numerous in those early days. Some were successful. Most were not.

In 1859 Topeka's founding father, Cyrus Kurtz Holliday, wrote and secured the passage of a bill creating the Atchison and Topeka Railroad Co. Its name was changed by charter amendment, in 1863, to the present-day Atchison, Topeka and Santa Fe Railway Co.

Like many early Kansas promoters, Holliday believed the fortunes of the state, his community, and himself depended on rail traffic. He was an incorporator of numerous railroads such as the Sedgwick and Cimarron Valley Railroad Co.; the Topeka, Cottonwood and Walnut Valley Railway Co.; and the Leavenworth, Oskaloosa and Topeka Railway Co., but found success mainly with the "Santa Fe."

In 1864 the Kansas Legislature approved a bill which permitted railroads to acquire additional lands within 20 miles of their line in lieu of lands already held by settlers. Counties also were authorized to vote subsidies of $200,000 to assist the railroads in their construction projects.

Initially taking advantage of the legislation were four railroads including the Santa Fe and the Leavenworth, Lawrence and Fort Gibson, which was to head south into Indian territory. A later, more ambitious plan projected Galveston, Texas, on the Gulf of Mexico, as the railroad's end-of-the-line.

The story of the LL&FG is one that typifies the difficulties these new railroads had getting started. Like the Santa Fe the line had a prestigious patron, James Lane, Kansas' first senator. He also was the railroad's first president.

Lane went to the voters of Douglas and Franklin counties and secured nearly $500,000 to build the LL&FG. Since the value of the bonds was estimated to be only half of their face value, the State of Kansas guaranteed to bring them up to full value.

Working under a tight deadline because Franklin County voters had set a precedent by stipulating that the railroad be completed within one year for the bonds to pay off, the LL&FG hired 450 workers. Four hundred of them were Chinese who earned 20 cents a day. The other 50 were Civil War veterans who got 75 cents a day, or one dollar if they had a horse.

In the spring of 1867 the workers began cutting down trees in the wilderness to obtain wood for ties and bridges. In June the railroad ordered its locomotives, rails, and tie plates from Liverpool, England. Because the American Civil War had ended just two years earlier, these materials were not readily available from U.S. manufacturers.

In September the equipment, including a locomotive, arrived in Lawrence on the north side of the Kaw River. The workers spent two months building a temporary bridge to get the locomotive to the south bank. That completed, they began laying track in earnest. The crews labored in two shifts around the clock. Night work was made possible with the aid of the locomotive's brilliant headlight.

The Santa Fe railroad is the largest single rail operation in the state. Photo by Bob Barrett

On December 30, two miles of track remained to be laid. Track workers, or "gandy dancers," hurriedly placed the tracks on top of the frozen ground and, although the train weaved as it followed the temporary rails into the town of Ottawa, the Leavenworth, Lawrence and Fort Gibson Railroad Co. met the imposed deadline. The rail sections were made permanent the next spring.

The railroad later went through several name changes and a bankruptcy before the AT&SF purchased it in 1880. The line was abandoned in the 1960s.

Although Santa Fe company headquarters are now located in Chicago, the railroad maintains a highly visible presence in Kansas. Its 1,079 miles of main line and 1,401 miles of branch line make it the largest single rail operation in the state. It also has numerous offices in Topeka and a large shop for car repairs.

Gone are the days when the Santa Fe ran such deluxe passenger liners as the Texas Chief, the Super Chief, and the El Capitan through Kansas. Semiretired is the Navajo boy caricature "Chico," who urged rail travelers to take "Santa Fe All The Way." The last of the line's passenger trains pulled into Chicago's Dearborn Station on May 2, 1971, the day after Amtrak commenced its operations.

Freight hauling pays the railroad's bills these days and determines profit and loss. It's big business.

Santa Fe transports more than 30 million tons of coal, farm products, food and kindred products, chemical and allied products, and other goods through the state yearly. That ranks second to Union Pacific/Missouri Pacific, which moves an average of more than 70 million tons of commodities in Kansas annually.

Other rail carriers transporting significant tonnage here include the Kansas City

The Santa Fe ships food, chemicals, coal, farm products, and automobiles and ranks second in Kansas to Union Pacific/Missouri Pacific which specializes in transporting commodities. Photo by Jim Shippee. Courtesy, Unicorn Stock Photos

Southern, 13 million tons; the Missouri-Kansas-Texas (MKT) and the Southern Pacific, 9 million tons each; the Denver & Rio Grande, 5 million tons; and the Burlington Northern, Oklahoma-Kansas-Texas, and Norfolk & Western railroads, more than one million tons each.

Several Kansas short line railroads also have been successful freight haulers for many years. The Garden City Western Railway has 14 miles of main line, and the Hutchinson Northern Railroad, five miles.

Newcomers are the Southeast Kansas Railroad, which bought 71 miles of main line from the Missouri Pacific between Coffeyville, Chetopa, and Cherokee, and the Kyle Railroad.

Based in the north-central Kansas community of Phillipsburg, the Kyle RR has approximately 400 miles of main line from Limon, Colorado, east to Clay Center. It acquired the route following the demise of the Rock Island Railroad and unsuccessful tries by other companies to make it profitable.

Rick Cecil, vice president of operations and general manager for the Kyle RR, recalls that his company took over the line in 1982 on a lease/purchase arrangement.

"A local newspaperman, the late 'Huck' Boyd, joined with a group of area shippers to form an organization called the Mid-States Port Authority," Cecil says. "They contacted us at our corporate offices which, at the time, were in San Diego. The Port Authority was aware of our success operating short line railroads from Tennessee to Hawaii—we have about 10 of them—and, in short, asked our management what it'd take for us to come here and operate their rail system."

In the interim period, while the Kyle Railroad and Mid-States Port Authority negotiated, the two parties entered into a month-to-month lease agreement. Service began following approval of the Rock Island's trustee and authorization from the Interstate Commerce Commission.

A final purchase agreement was consummated in 1984. Low-interest loans to upgrade the line were secured under the Railroad Revitalization and Rehabilitation Act and from the state. Bond issues were approved and the Kyle RR provided some matching funding.

"The port authority got the loans for a 20-year span and, essentially, what we have done is provide the guarantees for those loans," Cecil continues. "With the money, which was just under $10 million, we were able to restore and replace track and bring the railroad's operating speeds up from 5-10 mph to 35 mph, except in some low-density areas."

Kyle RR employment currently fluctuates between 75 and 100 persons. The figure is higher during the grain harvest season. By implementing a number of cost reduction practices without jeopardizing safety, the Kyle RR is making a profit on its Kansas-Colorado line.

The railroad maintains crew bases at Goodland, Phillipsburg, and Belleville. Two-man teams operate in what Cecil calls "conveyor belt fashion." Cecil explains:

Each team meets halfway between the train's point of origin and its next destination. Then they exchange cabs and return home. This practice saves us money that would be spent on accommodations, food, and wages if each team made the complete trip and "deadheaded" or overnighted. Our employees like the arrangement because they can spend more time with their families.

Cecil says the Kyle RR also got rid of the "antiquated train order arangement where papers would be issued saying this crew meets with this crew at this time and so forth." Now it operates under a method called DTC (direct train control).

"It's the railroad's answer to air traffic controllers," Cecil emphasizes. "What we have is a radio system manned by a dispatcher, 24 hours a day. The dispatcher can talk with any one crew, at any time, wherever they're at on our system.

"We've segmentized the entire line into certain blocks. Before a train crew can move from one block to another they must get authorization from the dispatcher. Permission is given only if it's safe for them to operate in the next block." He adds that the system also is ideal for track crews. They have a better idea of where train crews are at all times and don't have to spend hours waiting for a train that's been delayed.

The Kyle RR also has found a lucrative market in the leasing of its rolling stock to other railroads.

"We have 45 locomotives, and are acquiring additional units," Cecil says, "but that's misleading. We don't use them all.

"We're into a new venture—a peripheral business of buying older locomotives, restoring them at our Phillipsburg facility, and leasing the units to bigger railroads like the Burlington Northern, Southern Pacific, and Union Pacific who have a shortage of them."

Cecil points out that his railroad has been able to do this only because of the high quality of the workers the Kyle RR employs in Kansas.

"We've hired a couple of journeymen mechanics and electricians from other railroads and have a very aggressive apprenticeship program," he emphasizes. "We're ecstatic with our local employees and the quality of work they give us, not only in this refurbishing operation, but in our overall track and train service operation. I would think that this has to be one of the best-operating railroads in the country, and that includes among our other Kyle short lines."

Another Kyle RR cost-cutting measure is the continuing leasing of hopper cars (instead of buying them) to meet its heavily fluctuating needs.

"A new covered hopper costs roughly $50,000," Cecil notes, "and, depending on the season, our requirements are for 500 to 2,000 cars. We don't have the capital structure to build our own fleet, nor can we justify keeping all those cars around."

Cecil says that the Kyle RR and Mid-States Port Authority have a good working relationship.

"They've given us a lot of autonomy," he concludes. "In turn we've been able to give them, and our customers, the quality of service they want and need."

Throughout Kansas, both urban and rural areas are provided with excellent rail service. Due to the abundance of track mileage in the state, over 110 communities are served by more than one railroad. In those towns where straight interchanges are available, reciprocal switching agreements are possible between railroads.

An important part of the transportation system, about 12 railroad companies operate over 6,000 miles of track in the state. Photo by Arni Katz

Kansas' manufacturing sector, which includes the electrical industry, provides employment for 15 percent of the state. Photo by Aneal Vohra. Courtesy, Unicorn Stock Photos

7

Thomas Alva Edison introduced his light bulb to the world in 1879, but even in the early 1900s it was only used in a small percentage of American homes. Electricity at the flip of a switch, or the tug of a chain, was still in its infancy when the twentieth century began.

It was Wichita businessman William Coffin Coleman's products that provided much of the illumination in the nation's rural areas well into the 1930s. His Coleman lantern helped America's farmers extend their work days and turn this country into the agricultural giant it is today.

The Coleman Company continues to have an impact on developing countries and industrial nations alike. Its name has become synonymous throughout the world with quality and reliable outdoor and recreational products. Coleman lanterns are used in remote jungle hospitals, huts, and schools as well as at weekend retreats in every state. More than one million of them are made each year including single- and double-mantle versions fueled by gasoline, propane, or kerosene or operated by batteries.

During World War II the U.S. Army challenged The Coleman Company to design a stove that would burn any type of fuel on the battlefield, work at 60 degrees below and 125 degrees above zero, and be no larger than a quart-size milk bottle. The stove it developed was called by renowned war correspondent Ernie Pyle "one of the two most important pieces of noncombat equipment to come out of the war." The other was the jeep.

MADE IN KANSAS

After the war The Coleman Company revolutionized the cooler industry by inventing a "bubble machine" that permitted the molding of a plastic tub in one piece, thus making the galvanized iron coolers of the day obsolete. The process involved heating the plastic material, putting air pressure underneath, and blowing a big bubble, just like a soap bubble. This resulted in an exact thickness all around. After the plastic cooled, a plunger was used to turn the bubble inside out and form it into the interior of a cooler.

The process vaulted the company into a leadership position in portable iceboxes. The application of the process to portable jugs had the same effect.

The Coleman Company remains a major Wichita, and Kansas, employer that continues to be guided by its founder's motto: "Nothing is really sold until it is delivering satisfactory service for the user." More than 100 million Coleman products are in use today.

On a smaller scale, Emporia's Hopkins Manufacturing Company introduced a product several years ago that had such phenomenal success one month that it outsold both Cabbage Patch dolls and Trivial Pursuit games at the height of their popularity.

In the 1930s William Coffin Coleman's lanterns extended the work day for area farmers. Today The Coleman Company markets a variety of outdoor products that are used around the world. Courtesy, The Coleman Company, Inc.

"Hoppy Bear Paw Ice Scrapers" encase an ice scraper in a warm, dry mitt. The hand is protected against wet and cold as it removes ice and snow from frosted windshields and windows of motor vehicles.

Originally introduced for the automotive market, the item became a hit with consumers purchasing gifts in the under $10 range. When demand peaked, Hopkins Manufacturing Company sold more than 5 million of the ice scrapers annually.

Hopkins improved on the original product from both cosmetic and performance standpoints to meet customers' demands for more attractive and functional ice scrapers. Handsomely etched art scenes were added to some blades and new chippers that break through heavy ice also were introduced.

Mitts with simulated-fur lining and imitation sheepskin were brought out. Even battery-powered, lighted versions were marketed. The ice scrapers continue to sell at a steady rate.

Innovative ideas from Kansas companies, like the aforementioned from Coleman and Hopkins, have altered both the complex and simplistic ways the world lives and conducts its business. There are few places on earth that one can travel to where a Kansas-made product hasn't been pressed into service.

THE AIRCRAFT INDUSTRY

Probably the most visible of Kansas' manufactured goods are the aircraft that roll from assembly lines in Wichita. Beech, Boeing, Cessna, and Learjet are

recognized names in the commercial and general aviation industry and among global air travelers.

Beech, Cessna, and Learjet are recognized names in the commercial and general aviation industry. Photo by Arni Katz

Beech Aircraft Corp. is a subsidiary of the Raytheon Co., which is listed by *Fortune* magazine as one of the 100 largest companies in America. It is a premier manufacturer of corporate aircraft.

Beech employs more than 5,400 persons at its Wichita plant and 300 at its Salina facility. There are 8,250 "Beechcrafters" internationally.

Among the aircraft Beech builds is the "Bonanza," which has the longest production run of any commercial aircraft. The first one made its debut in 1946 and nearly 16,000 have been sold since. Also in the lineup are the "Baron," the "King Air," the "Super King Air," the "King Air Exec-Liner 1900," and the 530-mph "Beechjet."

Beech's business jet was originally designed and built by Japan's Mitsubishi Heavy Industries. The Kansas company acquired the aircraft in 1985 and made a number of changes to it including the redesign of the interior. Production was shifted to Wichita and Salina in 1988.

The newest addition to the Beech inventory is the "Starship," a futuristic-looking aircraft that has state-of-the-art technology: composite materials which are lighter and stronger than aluminum, a variable sweep canard (a small wing near the nose), and tip-sails standing upright at the ends of the aft wing.

"Two pusher prop-fan engines are located above, and to the rear of, the aft wing," says Beech spokesperson Pat Zerbe. "They are designed to propel the aircraft at over 400 mph."

Zerbe notes that the majority of Starship buyers are "upgrading from current turboprop aircraft."

"Other buyers include owners of small jets who want the short-field take-off and landing capabilities the Starship offers plus its increased cabin size and economy," she adds.

U.S. AIR

BOEING

Boeing Military Airplanes is the largest private employer in the State of Kansas. Its work force numbers more than 24,000 persons, more than double that of 1980.

Affiliated with the Boeing Co. of Seattle, Washington, the Wichita plant is the largest aerospace facility at a single site in the free world. The branch is housed in nearly 10 million square feet of company owned and leased, covered space.

Boeing Military Airplanes recently completed an expansion and modernization program costing in excess of one billion dollars. It currently has contracts for commercial and military aircraft modification and commercial aircraft assembly support, valued in the billions of dollars.

"We're in the midst of a KC-135 re-engine program for the U.S. Air Force," says Richard Hill of Boeing Military Airplanes' public relations department. "We're also doing the logistics for the B-1B bomber avionics program."

Hill emphasizes that his company is also performing extensive modifications on Air Force B-52 bombers and is its parent company's largest subcontractor for the 707, 737, 747, 757, and 767 designated aircraft.

"We build the nose sections for all of those planes," Hill points out, "plus 75 percent of the entire airframe of the 737. We also have designed and are building composite replacement wings for U.S. Navy A-6 aircraft."

Some of the other projects in which Boeing Military Airplanes is participating include the building of nacelles for commercial and military planes, providing avionics for the V-22 tilt-rotor airplane and the LHX helicopter, and unmanned aircraft systems development (drone research and manufacturing).

FACING PAGE TOP: A Boeing technician overhauls one of four engines on an Air Force KC-135 tanker at the Boeing Military Airplanes facility in Wichita. Courtesy, Boeing Military Airplanes

FACING PAGE BOTTOM: A rising star on the civil aviation scene, the Cessna Citation, pictured, is another in a long line of reliable aircraft produced by the Cessna Aircraft Company. Courtesy, Wallace Aircraft Division Cessna Aircraft Company. Courtesy, Tony Stone Worldwide

CESSNA

More than half of the aircraft now flying in non-Communist countries were manufactured by the Cessna Aircraft Co. Since 1927 the company has delivered more than 177,000 aircraft, including 24,000 twin-engine airplanes, 2,000 military jets, and 1,500 Citation business jets.

Five Citations have been delivered to the People's Republic of China, the first business jets sold in that country.

Cessna is also the only general aviation company which owns its own finance subsidiary, Cessna Finance Corp. CFC, one of the largest finance subsidiaries in the nation, has underwritten financing for more than 125,000 aircraft, valued at more than $5.4 billion.

It is estimated that 75 percent of all pilots flying today have received some of their instruction in Cessna aircraft. The company is the leader in pilot training through its worldwide network of Cessna Pilot Centers.

Cessna is owned by General Dynamics Corp. of St. Louis, one of America's largest defense contractors. The subsidiary operates two plants in Wichita and a Fluid Power Division in Hutchinson.

Fluid Power produces hydraulic components and systems for agricultural, construction, and industrial equipment.

Cessna's most popular aircraft models include the Citation and the "Caravan," which was introduced in 1985. The Caravan is a single-engine turboprop utility aircraft that can carry large cargo loads or up to 14 people. A specially designed version is being used by Federal Express, and the company is in the process of buying 199 more.

Others using the aircraft include the Royal Canadian Mounted Police, which has amphibious versions. It is the only single-engine aircraft certified by the U.S. Postal Service to carry the U.S. mail. A military version, the U-27A, has also been developed.

Cessna Aircraft Co.'s employment worldwide currently stands at about 6,000.

LEARJET

Learjet was spawned from an idea by Bill Lear in the late 1950s, when he envisioned a small, private, jet airplane for business travelers that would equal or exceed the performance of commercial jetliners. He was impressed with a Swiss fighter airplane known as the P-16 and set up a team of engineers in Switzerland to design what later became the Learjet, a name generic today with fast, reliable business transportation.

Lear relocated his operations from Switzerland to Wichita in 1962 and Learjet Corp. delivered its first Model 23 in 1964. The 500th Learjet went to the Mexican Navy in 1975. Number 1,000 was turned over to a customer in 1980.

Although the American market for Learjets has been sluggish in recent years, exports have picked up the slack. "The overseas market is blossoming for us," says Bill Robinson, vice president of corporate affairs for Learjet. "Major buyers have been Brazil, with 80 airplanes, Mexico with 45, West Germany with 26, and Canada with 23."

International applications for the aircraft include maritime patrol, electronic surveillance, special photo missions, and air ambulance service.

Prices for Learjets are in the $3.25-$6.2 million range.

"All of our aircraft are capable of crossing the United States with one stop," Robinson continues, "which makes them ideal for executive use."

The Learjet model 55C has a larger cabin than models 31 and 35. It also has a walk-in lavatory. All models can transport six to eight passengers at a cruise speed of 535 mph.

"Learjets also are seeing military service in the United States," Robinson notes. "The Air Force has 70 of them and the Air National Guard has four. The military designation is C-21A."

Learjet Corp. is a unit of Integrated Resources, Inc. of New York. The company employs 1,200 persons at its more than 900,000 square feet of facilities in Wichita and another 575 at a Tucson, Arizona, branch.

GENERAL MANUFACTURING ECONOMY

According to the 1988 statistics provided by the Kansas Department of Human Resources, manufacturing provides employment for more than 175,000 Kansans, or slightly more than 15 percent of the state's work force. Only wholesale and retail trade, government, and services employ more of the state's workers.

Kansas' manufacturing sector is composed of 10 major product categories. In durable goods, transportation equipment is the leader followed by machinery, including electrical; fabricated metal products; stone, clay, and glass products; and primary metal industries.

Food and kindred products lead the nondurable goods category and are followed by printing, publishing, and allied industries; chemicals and allied products; petroleum refining and related industries; and apparel and other finished goods.

Industrial growth has resulted from both the attraction of new manufacturers and the expansion of existing ones. During this decade the five industrial categories creating the most jobs through new manufacturers were food products, machinery, electrical equipment, lumber products, and fabricated metal products. In that same period the five industrial categories creating the most jobs through existing manufacturers were transportation equipment, food products, rubber and plastics, electrical equipment, and machinery.

Expansion, construction, and renovation are common sights throughout the state. Photo by Jeff Hetler. Courtesy, Unicorn Stock Photos

TRANSPORTATION

In the transportation field, General Motors operates a huge automobile assembly plant in the Fairfax Industrial District of Kansas City. Both Chevrolet and Pontiac automobiles are manufactured there.

One Kansas-made Pontiac, the Grand Prix SE, was named *Motor Trend* magazine's 1988 "Car of the Year."

A number of smaller companies, like Collins Industries, Inc., build bodies for various vehicles. Collins assembles ambulances, funeral coaches, limousines, small school buses, and small transit buses in Hutchinson.

Lawrence's Brown Cargo Van, Inc., manufactures truck van bodies and van kits. The Broce Manufacturing Co. of Dodge City markets its self-propelled highway brooms internationally.

Chance Industries, Inc., of Wichita, is undoubtedly the most diversified of Kansas' transportation manufacturers. The company has provided amusement rides to carnivals and theme parks since 1961. It also builds replicas of turn-of-the-century streetcars that are popular conveyances in many cities where real trolleys no longer operate.

"They're built on a heavy-duty transit bus chassis," says Richard Chance, company president, "and run on rubber tires."

Chance also has introduced the "Ameribus," a revolutionary approach to the nation's urban transit needs. The 29-foot, 30-passenger vehicle contains a "Rapid Transfer PM System" that permits a power module, which includes the coach's engine, transmission, and all related components, to be removed and replaced in less than an hour.

"Instead of investing in spare buses to use during scheduled maintenance, a transit company can cut costs dramatically by just buying a few extra power modules," Chance says. "With our product there's no need to have 12 buses in order to keep 10 running. Another plus is that the savings realized can benefit taxpayers who heavily subsidize the transit market."

Chance Industries' latest amusement ride is a newly designed Ferris wheel. "It's 27 meters tall, or approximately 10 stories, and hauls 120 passengers in six-person gondolas," Chance notes. "It also has 6,000 lights on it. Our 'wheel' is the largest to be manufactured in the United States since George Ferris built the first one for the World's Fair, in Chicago, in 1893."

MACHINERY

Kansas is an agricultural state and, as such, many of the machine industries within its borders manufacture products with rural ties.

Hay & Forage Industries, in Hesston, builds self-propelled hay and forage equipment. The company employs more than 1,100 workers in the south-central Kansas community.

Seymour Foods, in Topeka, manufactures egg-breaking machines capable of breaking and separating 30,000 eggs per hour. The equipment is used by companies like Kraft and Sara Lee. Seymour Foods has only one competitor in the world, a Danish company, and consequently does an excellent export business. Its egg washing and drying machines are also being adapted to a new market. Sporting goods manufacturers have found them ideal for preparing golf balls for painting.

Wenger Manufacturing occupies one-and-a-half square blocks of downtown Sabetha (population 2,286) and employs 130 persons. Sixty percent of its machinery is sold in foreign countries.

"We supply equipment to the food and feed industries for production of a wide variey of items," says Galen Rokey, manager of Wenger's Technical Research Center. "These include pet foods; aquatic foods for shrimp, fish, eel, and crawfish; instant pastas and rice; textured soy proteins; cereals; snacks; and breading, including the Oriental-style variety used for coatings by fast-food chains."

Rokey points out that his employer also is heavily involved in the industrial conversion of cellulose into sugars and other by-products. "Some of the raw materials that were formerly considered waste, like soybean hulls and oat hulls, are converted to dietary fiber by our extrusion equipment," he continues. "A bleaching process removes colors, 'off' flavors and odors, and enhances the product from health and nutritional aspects."

Major Far Eastern clients of Wenger Manufacturing are Japan, Taiwan, and the People's Republic of China.

"The Asians are particularly interested in the equipment we build in the aquatic feed and textured soy protein lines," Rokey says. "In Europe, the United Kingdom and Scandinavian countries buy a lot of instant pasta, breading, and aquatic feed production equipment."

Rokey notes that Wenger's Technical Research Center is the largest food-extrusion pilot plant in the world.

"We derive three advantages from having this facility at our home office," he says. "First, we're able to demonstrate to potential clients our various equipment systems. Secondly, we can develop new products here for our existing clientele and work closely with our manufacturing arm to build them. Lastly, as a pilot plant we can conduct our own research and development."

Hundreds of other Kansas businesses manufacture "ag" related products ranging from alfalfa pellets to farm implement carriers, pet foods to saddles, and bulk storage tanks to steel roofing. The economies of many small communities, like Durham with its Donahue Corp. (which builds stock trailers, hydraulic bale loaders, and other items), are tied to them. Often, they're the only company in town.

HARVESTING NATURAL RESOURCES

Kansas' mineral production significantly impacts the state's economy. All but two of the state's 105 counties have active extraction industries. According to the Kansas Geological Survey:

The estimated total value of mineral production in 1985 was $2.88 billion. Listed in descending order of value—crude oil, natural gas, and natural gas liquids account for 90 percent of the total value.

Important industries relying on the extensive fuel reserves are nitrogen fertilizer plants, natural gas plants, liquefied petroleum gas plants and those petroleum refineries producing lubricating oils, greases and paving mixtures as well as petroleum by-products.

Other important minerals include salt. The Carey, Cargill, and Morton companies produce a variety of salt products at their Hutchinson mines and plants. American Salt Co. has an operation in Lyons, and Independent Salt Co. mines rock salt in Kanopolis.

In southeast Kansas, Monarch Cement Co. makes portland and masonry cements in Humboldt. Ash Grove Cement Co. has a plant in nearby Chanute. Clemens Coal processes washed coal in Pittsburg.

Gold Bond Products taps the mineral wealth beneath the red bluffs and cedar-covered canyons of Barber County. The harvest of a huge deposit of gypsum, formed from precipitation of calcium sulfate in what was once a vast inland sea, provides jobs for one out of 10 persons in Medicine Lodge, the county seat.

Gold Bond is a subsidiary of the National Gypsum Co. It operates a gigantic mine-quarry-manufacturing complex in the community and in nearby Sun City. The industry employs 215 persons and another 100 or more provide support services to the local facility.

Wallboard for use in building and remodeling projects is Gold Bond Products' main manufactured item. Although actual production figures are confidential, plant manager Jack Dooley says an output of 350 million square feet of wallboard annually is a "ball park figure." The company also manufactures five-sixteenths-inch Duraform wallboards for the large mobile home manufacturing industry in Kansas and elsewhere, plus plaster and joint treatment.

"Despite erratic construction trends nationwide, demand for our manufactured goods has been steady," Dooley emphasizes. "We market in Denver, Kansas City, and the Southwest, and places in between like Wichita. These metropolitan areas are growing and the building activity there is keeping our production constant."

Gypsum mining is not done with picks and shovels nor does it require a mammoth crane. Rather, it's a clean-up operation after a controlled explosion.

Dooley says the process of making wallboard is a fairly simple one. "We run the rock into the mill from our stockpiles, pre-dry it in a rock dryer, then send it through crushers again until it's reduced to powder. The next step is to cook it until we get a certain percent of the moisture out of it. At that point we call it stucco or plaster of paris," he explains.

"Calcination is a heat process for the moisture extraction. We take chemical water out of the material and then, at the board plant, reintroduce water to make the finished product."

According to Dooley, the wallboard business is very competitive. He estimates there are three or four large companies in the business nationwide, including Georgia-Pacific's facility in Blue Rapids, plus 10 or 12 independents.

"We manufacture more products than probably any other wallboard plant," he says. "The white rock we have is so pure we even make plaster and distribute it to our other facilities in the United States. We call this product, 'Unikal.'

"We're also unique to the industry in that we have a quarry and mine near our plant," he adds. "Most others have to transport their raw materials from great distances including Nova Scotia and Mexico."

Dooley sees a bright future for Gold Bond Products in Barber County. The company has access to gypsum reserves that will provide a plentiful supply of the mineral for hundreds of years.

NAME RECOGNITION

Kansas has a number of nationally known companies, in addition to those already mentioned, operating plants in the state. Here's a sampling of these companies, along with descriptions of what they manufacture:

Bendix/King—*Located in Olathe and Paola, it designs and produces aircraft communi cation, navigation, and flight control systems.*
Boise Cascade Corp.—*Fiber cans and tubes are manufactured at its Edwardsville plant.*
Clorox Co.—*Makes cat box filler in Kansas City.*
Colgate-Palmolive Co.—*Its Kansas City operation manufactures soap, cleansers toothpaste, glycerin, and detergents.*
Fuller Brush Co.—*Makes household and industrial products including mops, brushes, brooms, and chemicals at its Great Bend factory.*
Gates Rubber Co.—*Produces hydraulic, rotary drill, and industrial hose in Iola.*
Hallmark Cards Inc.—*Greeting cards, gift wrap, stationery, puzzles, and other products are manufactured in Topeka, Leavenworth, Lawrence, and Osage City. The company's Binney & Smith subsidiary in Winfield produces crayons, artists' paints, and related products.*
Procter & Gamble Mfg. Co.—*Makes soap, industrial chemicals, and detergents in Kansas City.*
Purina Mills Inc.—*Has feed manufacturing operations in Wichita, Liberal, and Leoti.*
Quaker Oats Co.—*Manufactures pet foods in Lawrence and Topeka.*

From small businesses, major industries grow. The four companies profiled below are making significant contributions to the economies of the cities they're located in and are important to the state's overall manufacturing picture. Each has established itself in its field of expertise and looks forward to continued prosperity.

ART'S TATER CHIPS

Nearing 60 years of age, Art Kyburz is the new kid on the block in the Kansas potato chip industry. In a 32,000-square-foot plant in Walton, Kyburz and his wife, Mary, fry Art's Tater Chips, a tasty snack that has grocers making room for it on their shelves.

"That's almost an impossibility these days," Kyburz emphasizes. "Stores only have so much space to allot for certain types of products and what's available usually goes to the major manufacturers who have the big bucks to pay for it. We don't have

A household name, Hallmark Cards, Inc., has manufacturing plants in Topeka, Leavenworth, Lawrence, and Osage City. Photo by Arni Katz

the money to compete that way so we've gone to the people, created a demand, and used our popularity to get inside the doors."

To introduce Art's to Kansans, the Kyburzs became hucksters on weekends and evenings. At home shows, travel shows, or anywhere they could "work" a crowd, the two passed out free samples from their small booth. They still do.

Art's first chips weren't as eagerly received as Kyburz thought they would be. Business was so bad he almost "closed the doors" in 1983. "People won't buy a lard-fried chip here," he says, "so I made a decision to fry with 100 percent peanut oil. It's cholesterol-free and produces good-tasting chips. Sales have risen steadily and we've had to move to this new plant from north Wichita."

Kyburz claims customers get more potatoes for their money in his bags than they do in those of most other brands. "The major potato chip manufacturers usually fry their potatoes faster, and in hotter oil that we do," he emphasizes. "That way the potatoes don't shrink as much as they do with my slow cook process. Their packaged product weighs the same as ours but I have to use more potatoes to achieve that weight."

Art's now sells nacho chips in addition to no-salt, regular, and jalapeno varieties. Dutch-style and mini pretzels and barbecued pork rinds also have been added to the product line.

AMERICAN WALNUT CO.

John R. Worrell and Ed Grasso bought the American Walnut Co. of Kansas City in 1986, convinced they could do a better job of running it than its former owners. Employment at the sawmill was at an all-time low of 17, and the business' inventory had turned over only once during the year.

Less than 12 months later, 50 persons were drawing a paycheck at American and the warehouses had been replenished three times.

Worrell and Grasso began sawing oak and hackberry in addition to walnut. Both woods are in demand overseas. Much of the white oak is shipped to Europe, where it's made into finished furniture for the domestic market there. Red oak is transported to Taiwan, where it also is made into finished furniture but for sale in the United States. Most of the hackberry goes to Japan as a substitute for their own depleted supplies of a wood called sen.

"Hackberry is a light-colored wood as is sen," Grasso says. "Its grains are clear and it can be stained to look like other woods. We're selling 50,000 board feet a month to the Japanese."

For domestic consumption, American Walnut is producing 2,500 fully outlined gunstocks daily for the Ithaca Gun Co. in Ithaca, New York.

"We added a second mill here in 1988 and doubled production," Grasso notes. "However our problem still remains meeting demand fast enough."

American Walnut buys 4 million feet of logs annually plus more than a million feet of lumber. The majority comes from Kansas, Iowa, and Missouri. The company is keenly sensitive to the environment. To assure an uninterrupted inventory of walnut logs, five seedlings are planted for every mature tree harvested.

Waste products from the mill are used in a custom-built steam boiler that provides all the fuel for American Walnut's kilns and other equipment. The remainder is sold for mulch.

BALDERSON COMPANIES

Balderson Inc., a Wamego manufacturer of accessory construction machinery and equipment, exports 20 percent of its output. The Soviet Union is Balderson's single largest overseas customer.

Company president Clark Balderson says the Russians like the manufacturer's attachments, such as bulldozer blades and scoops, because they hold up in the intense cold at their huge mining and timber harvesting operations in Siberia.

Balderson Inc.'s origins are tied to winter weather. Its first products were snow plows, manufactured in 1930, for the Kansas State Highway Department.

In the early 1980s, while exports were up, Balderson's domestic sales dropped. "Our competition was building specialty blades for use in our two largest stateside forestry markets, Georgia and Washington," Balderson says. "At the same time we were trying to cover both areas with a single multipurpose blade."

The Balderson Inc. staff decided that the best method of combating the competition was to purchase a small competitor and learn the area's needs from the people who were already there.

" The philosophy we've adopted is to go into a region and find a small factory to buy, in the 10,000 to 15,000 square foot range," Balderson points out. "The people there know their market and we know how to build the products. Both operations complement each other."

Balderson Inc. now has subsidiaries in Florida and Washington. They are collectively known as the Balderson Companies. Affiliates are in Australia, Canada, and the Netherlands.

The specialized nature of the Balderson Companies' accessory products doesn't lend itself to being manufactured by much automated equipment. Most of the steel fabrication must be done by hand.

"Ours is a very people-oriented business," Balderson says. "Our employees consider themselves a part of this company, not just workers for it. Quality control is not a major problem here. Balderson employees won't settle for second best."

HOLIDAY MANSION

Holiday Mansion builds houseboats at its Salina factory like Rolls-Royce makes cars—by hand and from scratch. Three of its 80 employees work solely at inspecting the houseboats to make sure they're the finest in their class that money can buy.

"We don't turn out any seconds," says company president Stan Byquist. "It is important to us that the customer get a high quality product at a reasonable price."

Holiday Mansion makes six models of houseboats, from 36 to 49 feet in length. They sell for up to $150,000 each. Order one now and, at a one-a-day production rate, take delivery in about three months.

The company's biggest market is along the eastern seaboard of the United States and the Florida Gulf Coast. Byquist thinks Japan is also going to be a good market. Holiday Mansion's representative there sold six boats during the first 60 days the office was open for business. Customers have also come from Canada, Mexico, Kuwait, England, Saudi Arabia, and Germany.

According to Byquist his company, which has existed for several decades, started "going places" in 1982 when it "revolutionized" the industry with an aft-cabin design that permitted two bedrooms and two baths in a 38-footer.

"Nobody else had done that before in anything less than a 45-footer," Byquist notes. "Potential customers looked at us, loved that we could provide the amenities of a larger houseboat at less price and in a more maneuverable model, and bought. Sales escalated by 40 percent the year after we brought it out."

The company hasn't looked back.

"More people are starting to live on houseboats, full time," Byquist says, "and there are many condominium marinas being developed where before, houseboats were prohibited. The market future looks excellent!"

Fashion designers, professional seamstresses, tailors, and amateur sewers rely on McCall's patterns to "fit" their needs. Photo by Arni Katz

It's the beginning of another day at this office complex in Overland Park. Photo by Keith Philpott

8

Jerry Fornelli wasn't sure how he and his family would like living in Kansas. A lifelong resident of the Chicago area, he had been named distribution center manager for Stanley Hardware, which required a move to Lenexa.

"I was surprised when I got here," Fornelli recalls. "It was a lot nicer than what I had expected . . . which was a flat land with lots of wheat fields."

He says that his wife and children also were skeptical of the impending move.

"We had some friends who lived here 10 to 15 years ago and they kept telling her they spent their whole summer in the basement dodging tornadoes," Fornelli says. "The children's Illinois schoolmates had them convinced that their new home would be on a farm."

Instead, the Fornellis live in an upscale surburban area of Kansas City. And tornadoes haven't been a problem.

"We have a nice home," Fornelli says, "and taxes are a lot cheaper than in Illinois. The schools are good and the pace is a little slower here. My family has adapted well."

Fornelli's situation is similar to those related by a number of plant managers statewide. "Outsiders" tend to think of Kansas as lacking cities and the cultural and social amenities that go with them, they note. Some move here reluctantly. Once in the state, however, many of these same people express dismay when asked to transfer elsewhere.

A CLIMATE FOR COMMERCE

Businesses, too, have found the "good life" in Kansas. Distribution centers, like Stanley Hardware, have sprung up in the state. Manufacturing growth has rebounded from the effects of the national recession of 1981 and 1982. The state's 1988 unemployment rate was 4.8 percent, 0.7 percent below the national average.

What is Kansas doing to attract new businesses and to retain those already operating in the state? Stanley Hardware's decision to consolidate two out-of-state distribution centers at one location in Lenexa is a good example. According to Fornelli:

We looked on both sides of the state line [Kansas and Missouri] before choosing this site. Influencing our decision was the fact that Kansas is a Right-to-Work state and Missouri is not. Also, this area has a good employable work force with a good work ethic. Further, we were impressed with the assistance we had from the Lenexa Chamber of Commerce, the Kansas Department of Commerce, and the Kansas Department of Human Resources. The Lenexa Chamber ran a recruiting ad for us, and sorted through more than 300 resumes. We used the Department of Human Resources' offices to conduct interviews.

Fornelli hired an outside consultant through Johnson County Community College, and orientation sessions were held in a building leased with matching funds provided by the Kansas Department of Commerce through its Kansas Industrial Training program. At the sessions, Stanley Hardware officials introduced themselves and their company and administered a series of job aptitude tests.

Matching funds for hiring and training the new employees were provided by the Kansas Department of Commerce. A sample factory was set up and training sessions were conducted in a job-like setting.

In return, Kansas became Stanley Hardware's distribution center for 22 states.

Walmart's experimental HyperMart in Topeka draws a large crowd. Photo by Arni Katz

The company's former Chicago and Dallas operations were combined into one 115,000-square-foot facility that distributes hinges, wire goods, handles, pulls, casters, and other products, more than 2,500 items. The distribution center also is the prime storage area for a new line of sliding and bi-fold door hardware shipped nationwide.

Fornelli is the only one of the center's more than 30 employees who wasn't hired locally.

"Locating in Kansas was a good business move for us," adds Fornelli. "We're a growing company and this is a growing area. We have a quality and reliable staff, an interstate highway less than a mile away, and the value of our land has appreciated since we opened our doors."

CALLING OUT THE CAVALRY

The private sector is encouraged to assist the Kansas Department of Commerce, and other state and local agencies, in economic development promotion. One of the unique ways it does this is through an organization known as the Kansas Cavalry.

Since 1973 the "Cavalry" has been the business reconnaissance arm and economic development patrol of the State of Kansas. It is charged, by the governor, with the mission of fostering and safeguarding the "good and prosperous growth of our State by lending a professional touch to the hosting of industrial prospects and other visiting businesspersons."

The Kansas Cavalry was conceived by the late Governor Robert Docking, a Democrat; former lieutenant governor David Owen, a Republican; and Terence Scanlon, then director of the Kansas Department of Economic Development, the Kansas Department of Commerce's predecessor. They had just returned from leading a delegation of Kansans to Japan on a reverse investment mission.

"The concept had worked on the trip to the Orient and these three reasoned that it could work closer to home," says Harland Priddle, Secretary of Commerce for Kansas. "They thought it was time that private citizens of the state became more involved in its economic development."

Governor Docking asked Overland Park banker Ben Craig to be the Cavalry's first commanding general. Between 50 and 75 charter members, some personally recruited by the governor, comprised the first "Troop."

Membership in the Kansas Cavalry has continued to grow, and more than 270 manufacturers, retailers, chamber of commerce and industrial development executives, and other businesspeople make up the organization's current complement.

"This is one of the premier groups of its kind in the country," Priddle continues. "Members volunteer their time, and travel at their own expense, to make personal calls on selected industries and to promote Kansas' positive attributes to interested companies."

Missions have been national and international in scope. Cities in New York, Illinois, Pennsylvania, Taiwan, Japan, and Germany are among those that have been visited by the Cavalry.

"Businesspeople from around the world have been impressed by the involvement of these individuals," states Dick Nichols, the Cavalry's present commanding general. "What better people are there to address the favorable business climate in Kansas than those who already are doing business here?"

Each year, at the Cavalry's annual encampment, a Kansas city is singled out for being outstanding in its industrial development efforts. Recognition is conferred by a Community Achievement Award presented by the governor. The Kansas Cavalry also acknowledges that the state's existing industry is vital to Kansas' economic health and is the key to a prosperous future. Centenarian Awards are presented to those industries that have operated in the state for 100 years.

Another program is Industry Appreciation Week. "The week-long observance is a way to say 'thank you' to companies here," says Nichols. "Members also exhort their communities to honor local industries with activities such as luncheons, tours, open houses, awards ceremonies, proclamations, and newspaper inserts."

KANSAS INC.

Kansas Inc. is a partnership between the State of Kansas and the private sector to improve economic development strategic planning, coordination, and evaluation for Kansas. Two-thirds of its annual $500,000 budget are funded by the state, and one-third by contributions from businesses and associations.

Authorized by the Kansas Legislature in 1986, Kansas Inc. works closely with the Kansas Department of Commerce, the Kansas Technology Enterprise Corporation, Kansas Venture Capital, Inc., and other major economic organizations to ensure that the state economy continues to grow. To accomplish this, says Charles R. Warren, Kansas Inc. president, focus and direction toward six pillars of strength are critical. The pillars are:

* *Entrepreneurial—The maintenance of a healthy climate for business and entrepreneurial environment.*

* *Capital Markets—Expanded capital markets for investment in Kansas companies.*

* *Infrastructure—Intelligent public investment in roads, water, sewers, and other capital needs.*

* *Human Capital—The knowledge and skills that people accumulate through education, training, and experience.*

* *Capacity Building—The ability for prompt and effective response and assistance by economic development organizations.*

* *Technology—The development, application, and transfer of technology to meet business needs.*

Four specific initiatives are implemented to achieve these goals. "Strategic planning, coordination, evaluation, and research are the keys to our programs," Warren says. "We conduct research using outside consultants, particularly from Kansas Regents institutions, and our own four-person staff. Kansas Inc. then recommends legislative or administrative action to produce a growing economy for the state."

Kansas Inc.'s 15-member board of directors consists of representatives from major Kansas industries, organized labor leaders, and legislative leaders. It meets regularly, nine times a year, in open sessions.

As president of Kansas Inc., Warren works closely with the governor as an advisor to the cabinet and participates in its meetings.

"Only one other state has a public/private partnership at this level," Warren continues, "but I think we'll be seeing many more of them in the future. They're almost a must to gain an advantage in the highly competitive economic development field."

Warren notes that "national" policy is now being made in economic development by state governments through their cumulative and consistent adoption of programs at the state level and without the intervention or influence of the federal government. In fact, he adds, this comes as a direct result of inaction or inattention by the federal government. According to Warren:

Historically, states have been in the development game for decades. Their involvement can be traced back to the canal building era of the 1850s. Today, with the exception of certain tax incentives, or depreciation, and job training programs, most state programs are not influenced directly by federal policies. Therefore, for a state like Kansas to continue to grow, it is incumbent that our actions in the economic development field be sound ones.

Our research agenda and policy recommendations seek to make Kansas a leader in future economic development. A major part of this process has been to identify issues in which Kansas Inc., through its research responsibilities, can have a significant impact.

Kansas Inc.'s future research projects will focus on:

Capital availability—How can the state ensure that sources of capital are available to job-generating entrepreneurs? In addition, a review of banking regulations and whether changes need to be made in the state's banking industry will be undertaken.

Small manufacturers—Who are they and what policy options targeting this group will create an environment conducive to their survival and expansion?

Increased exports of Kansas products—The global economy demands that states market goods internationally. This study will determine steps Kansas must take to increase its exports.

"These priorities are the product of a cooperative attempt to identify and rank key economic development issues," Warren says. "Kansas Inc. has consulted with

Owner Chuck Magerl is pictured here in his restaurant, part of the Free State Brewery in Lawrence. The homemade brews are sold only in the restaurant, and some claim it to be the best they have ever tasted. Photo by Arni Katz

members of the Kansas Legislature, local and state leaders, educators from a variety of academic disciplines, and private sector leaders in creating this agenda. All participants recognize that promotion of the interests of Kansas will benefit the organizations they represent in a way that multiplies their own efforts."

PRIMARY STATE DEVELOPMENT AGENCY

The Kansas Department of Commerce consists of six divisions whose collective responsibilities foster economic development through promotion of business, commerce, and industry. The divisions are Administration, Community Development, Existing Industry, Industrial Development, Trade Development, and Travel and Tourism.

The Community Development Division is responsible for creating an environment conducive to economic development in Kansas communities by providing grants, technical assistance, and information, enabling local leaders to deal with development issues and opportunities. Kansas is among the nation's leaders in implementing enterprise zone legislation of unparalleled flexibility, and the division gives technical assistance to cities and counties in local designation of the zones.

Other activities of the division include:

* *Community Technical Assistance to bridge the gap experienced by many communities desiring to improve their economic conditions, but lacking the technical expertise to do so effectively.*
* *Making recommendations to communities which seek to revitalize their downtown areas. The assistance is known as the Kansas Main Street Program.*
* *Overseeing the Kansas PRIDE Program, which provides incentives, recognition, and technical assistance for volunteer efforts in community improvement.*
* *Administering the Kansas Small Cities Community Development Block Grant (CDBG) Program, which makes Housing and Urban Development funds available to cities and counties for planning, community improvement projects, and economic development.*
* *The management of the new Rural Development Assistance Center.*
* *The Kansas Partnership Fund.*

The Division of Existing Industry Development promotes and encourages the growth, diversification, and retention of business and industry in Kansas. It has three primary programs. They are:

* *Identifying and addressing the needs of existing and start-up businesses in Kansas. The division coordinates a statewide business assistance network to channel businesses to appropriate resources for business planning, technical help, financing, or other business problems.*
* *The promotion, encouragement, and assistance of minority business operations through technical assistance in procurement and contracting, financing, business planning, and identification of business opportunities.*
* *The maintenance of six regional field offices to provide technical assistance to businesses, communities, and other development organizations.*

The Division of Travel and Tourism is responsible for increasing the number of visitors to Kansas, by promoting the state as a travel opportunity to both Kansans and non-Kansans alike.

White collar business, a classification not common when settlers first arrived in Kansas, is quite diversified and employs a large number of people in wholesale, retail, trade, manufacturing, government, and other service-oriented industries. Photo by Tom McCarthy. Courtesy, Unicorn Stock Photos

TRADE DEVELOPMENT

The Division of Trade Development encourages the export of Kansas products by creating opportunities for trade development and market research missions to international markets. It speaks the language of international business. On staff are individuals fluent in Chinese, German, Japanese, Spanish, Portuguese, and, of course, English. The division is one of 18 organizations in Kansas working at some facet of international trade promotion. Their common goal is to sell products from the state abroad.

Essential to the Trade Development Division's overseas promotion efforts are two offices, maintained by the state, in Tokyo, Japan, and Stuttgart, West Germany. Trade service contract representatives also are retained in Taipei, Taiwan; Bangkok, Thailand; Jakarta, Indonesia; Henan Province, China; Seoul, Korea; and Latin America (Colombia, Ecuador, Paraguay, and Peru).

The Trade Development Division employs several methods to introduce Kansas companies to the export scene. One is to initiate calls to the businesses, meet with key officials of the firms, and ask a number of questions that are designed to help the division's staff understand those companies and what overseas markets they'd like to enter.

At the Trade Development Division's headquarters in Topeka, a profile of the businesses and their products is made. The information is then forwarded to the state's overseas offices that can best assist in making a match of buyer and seller.

The Trade Development Division also hosts foreign businesspersons when they are in the state and conducts trade missions to other countries. In addition to European and Asian markets, the state agency is aggressive in South America.

DIFFICULT PROBLEM, EASY SOLUTION

Some Kansas ingenuity had to be employed to resolve a snag that developed in communications between businesses here and in Kansas' sister state, Henan Province, China.

For several years, two students from state universities were selected by committee, annually, to receive a small amount of funding authorized by the state legislature to act as commercial coordinators in Henan Province. They would spend a portion of their time taking courses in Chinese business and visiting with Chinese companies, but would spend the remainder of their time working for the Trade Development Division.

"Before their arrival we had a lot of telexes go unanswered," says Secretary of Commerce Priddle. "We were never sure whether the Chinese didn't get them, whether they got them and didn't understand them, or whether they got them and didn't understand how to reply. With the students, telexes were received by Kansans and answered by Kansans."

Unfortunately, the program has been temporarily discontinued due to the 1989 political unrest in China.

INDUSTRIAL DEVELOPMENT

The Industrial Development Division is responsible for the recruitment of new business and industry including manufacturing, warehousing/distributing, and service projects. The division's functions include domestic marketing and international development.

The international development section recruits new business investment from international sources. Direct investment, joint ventures, and licensing are solicited from corporations based in Europe, Asia, and Canada.

The domestic marketing section works with United States-based companies considering Kansas as a location for new business facilities. The section's marketing activities include space advertising, direct mail, and prospecting trips. Other activities include publishing "Developing Kansas," a quarterly development newsletter; administering the Kansas Industrial Training (KIT) Program; and managing the Kansas Cavalry Organization.

The KIT Program provides a comprehensive and flexible approach to industrial training. It addresses a firm's unique needs and specifications by permitting the company to decide how it wants to conduct that training.

Division specialists work with individual companies to formulate an overall training plan that covers training methods, instructors, trainee selection, training facilities, production schedules, and a program budget. Additionally, local educational agencies like community colleges and vocational technical schools are active program participants and offer the use of their facilities and staff expertise to meet training objectives.

The KIT Program pays negotiated costs of pre-employment, on-the-job, and

Safelite Glass belongs to a fraternity of industrial producers that continue to expand on Kansas' manufacturing base. Photo by Arni Katz

classroom training expenses that include instructor salaries; travel, meals, and lodging; videotapes, training manuals, and textbooks; supplies and materials; minor equipment; certain utility costs; and curriculum planning and development.

The Kansas Department of Human Resources also plays an important role in the employment and training process. Local employment and training offices throughout the state assist in recruiting, testing, and screening potential trainees in accordance with a company's hiring specifications.

The department, in cooperation with local private industry councils, also administers the statewide arm of the Job Training Partnership Act. JTPA offers a training cost reimbursement of up to 50 percent of an eligible employee's wages during the training period.

The KIT and JTPA programs can be used together or separately to develop a training program designed to meet the needs of virtually any new or expanding industry.

FISCAL ADVANTAGES

Kansas lawmakers have redefined job investment and tax credits in the state. Exemptions are offered on real and personal property taxes and sales tax paid on building materials and equipment.

By state constitutional decree, Kansas must maintain a balanced budget. Despite this, the state's corporate tax rate has remained constant since 1972.

Utilities generally are less expensive in the Sunflower State than in many other parts of the country. Kansas is one of only a handful of states with a positive energy balance. In the extreme southwestern corner of the state is the 4,800-square-mile Hugoton Gas Area, which contains one of the world's largest deposits of natural gas.

Consumption of natural gas in Kansas lags more than 60 percent behind

production. Consequently, most areas of the state have no marketing constraints on the sale of the fuel, even to large volume users.

FACING PAGE: A Johnson County high rise glistens in Corporate Woods at sunset. Photo by Keith Philpott

Costs per thousand cubic feet (mcf) of natural gas are commensurate with supplies. According to 1988 statistics from the Kansas Department of Commerce, users in the state paid an average $3.69 per mcf as compared to $4.80 for consumers in California, $5.23 for those in New York, and $4.58 for Illinois users. The mean price for consumption, at the national level, was $4.25.

Major natural gas companies serving Kansas, with no constraints on volume users, are Northwest Central Pipeline Corp.; Internorth, Inc.; KPL Gas Service; KN Energy, Inc.; ARKLA, Inc.; and Union Gas System.

Natural gas fuels almost 6 percent of the state's facilities, oil fuels less than half a percent, and electricity fuels most of the remainder.

Electric power rates are below the national average and the state's energy-generating capacity shows healthy reserves that exceed the national recommendation.

Nearly 80 percent of the electricity generated in Kansas comes from coal-fired plants. The state's close proximity to Wyoming, with its enormous supply of low-sulfur coal, results in inexpensive transportation costs for the fossil fuel. Some of the savings are passed on to consumers.

Wolf Creek Nuclear Plant—operated by Kansas Gas and Electric (KG&E), Kansas City Power and Light (KCP&L), and Kansas Electric Power Cooperative, Inc.—provides the rest of the state's electricity.

There are two major power suppliers in Kansas in addition to KCP&L and KG&E. They are KPL Gas Service and Western Power Division-Central Telephone & Utilities.

Southwestern Bell is the major telecommunications company in Kansas. It serves 95 percent of all homes and businesses in the state. Nearly 40 local independent telephone companies meet the needs of the remaining 5 percent.

More than 60 percent of Southwestern Bell's customers are connected to electronic switching systems that offer advanced business communication capabilities, plus custom calling features such as call forwarding, call hold, call waiting, conference calling, and speed calling. Many independents provide similar services.

Major telephone improvements currently under way in the state include the installation of digital call switching machines and fiber optic cables, and the upgrading of network capabilities through pair gain systems.

Digital switches and fiber optic cables transmit voice and data as pulses of pure light from tiny lasers. They offer greater transmission capacities and work at much higher speeds compared to conventional systems.

Pair gain technology increases the transmission capacity of existing copper cables and conditions them to carry digital computer data.

A Right-to-Work law, many incentives, stable taxation, abundant energy, and a work force with the right attitude are some of the advantages of doing business in Kansas.

The welcome mat is out for companies wishing to relocate to Kansas. Encouragement also is given to those companies that want to expand here. State agencies, private business, and a reliable and productive work force team together to make each venture as successful as possible. It pays to "set up shop" here. Kansas' climate for doing business is among the best—anywhere!

These flags represent the hard work that has made Kansas what it is today.
Photo by Bruce Mathews

PART

III

KANSAS' ENTERPRISES

By Judith Galas

Photo by Arni Katz

9

Kansas' energy, communication, and transportation providers keep products, information, and power circulating inside and outside the area.

NETWORKS

HIGH PLAINS PUBLISHERS, INC.

The *High Plains Journal* markets its products to plains farmers across the midsection of the country.

In the late 1860s the western-bound railroad made a temporary dead end in the depths of the High Plains of Kansas, just short of the Rocky Mountains. That is where Dodge City was born. As the dust from countless cattle drives settled on this untamed end-of-the-trail outpost, up sprang saloons, dance halls, and hotels—Boot Hill, Wyatt Earp, and the wild, wild West.

Though the dust from cattle drives has long since disappeared, huge beef-packing plants around Dodge City, countless irrigation rigs, and rolling wheat fields still attest to the agricultural roots of the High Plains. And perched on what might be called publishing hill, near the edge of this historic town, is the home of the *High Plains Journal*, a publication that understands the importance and growth of High Plains agriculture.

The *High Plains Journal* has always viewed its mission as serving the whole geographic market of the High Plains, rather than just a single state. That is why the publication serves more than 63,000 subscribers in Colorado, Kansas, Missouri, Nebraska, New Mexico, Oklahoma, Texas, and Wyoming. In fact, its latest promotional campaign touts the High Plains as "agriculture's 51st state."

Though it might seem that this area could support only a few types of agriculture, and that specialized vertical publications might better serve, Joe Berkely, publisher, disagrees. "While it is true that there are vertical markets in agriculture, our rancher-farmers on the High Plains are diversified—cattle, wheat, milo."

Cattle are a seasonal commodity for some High Plains producers. After grazing cattle on wheat, many producers harvest the wheat for grain. Other crop residues—corn or milo stalks—are utilized for cattle forage. "That's why the *High Plains Journal* is a diversified farm publication," explains Duane Ross, associate publisher. "We are different things at different times."

More than a century ago, in 1883, a weekly frontier newspaper began, the *Dodge City Democrat.* The publication's name changed from the *Democrat* to the *Dodge City Kansas Journal* and then to the *Dodge City Journal.*

In 1945 changes to the editorial approach to agriculture saw the circulation of the farmer's paper make its way out of Dodge City and into the surrounding area. Starting with a total of 132 subscribers, it has grown to 63,000. Berkely was one of the new owners. Compared to its current roster exceeding 150 employees, *High Plains* began small with five people. They wrote farm news, sold advertising, and printed and produced the paper.

Subscribers were quickly added by the early circulation drives. In 1949 the *High Plains Journal* name was adopted to reflect the agricultural geographic area that it served. In the early days it was a southwestern Kansas paper, then a northwestern edition was added. Later, eastern Kansas was given an edition. Expansion into surrounding states started

PUBLISHER'S HILL

Located on the crest of a hill on Wyatt Earp Boulevard at the eastern city limits of Dodge City, Kansas, the *High Plains Journal* does just about everything under one roof.

"You see, we're just about 300 miles from everywhere," says publisher Joe Berkely. If there is a service connected with any phase of publishing, the *High Plains Journal* probably does it in-house.

Editorial copy, classifieds, and ads are typeset on a massive in-house Compugraphics typesetting network and fed to a paste-up and production department. Separations are done, plates are made, and the printing is done on a web press in-house.

Outside wire news arrives over a satellite-receiver downlink that feeds directly into editorial computers. Special promotional pieces and commercial art are provided by the art department. Everything from local history books to genealogical journals are produced by the book division.

Ads may be prepared by the High Plains Journal Advertising Agency, policies sold by the High Plains Journal Insurance Agency, and much of the area business printing is provided by the High Plains Publishers commercial printing plant. And the telemarketing function of the organization provides a service to outside clients.

A new, large auditorium, complete with audiovisual equipment and catering facilities, is available to local agricultural businesses and associations free of charge. Visitors can enjoy the High Plains Journal Arboretum, the only one of its kind for hundreds of miles.

The necessity for self-sufficiency has created a versatile work force. "We all tend to get involved in all things that go on here," says Duane Ross, associate publisher. "When people come to work here, they plan to come and spend their lives," adds Berkely. "We communicate—we don't hide anything. That has built a good relationship between management and employees over a long period of time."

The 37-foot wheat sculpture in front of this publishing facility stands as a tribute to agriculture, and to the originality of determined people.

with Colorado, followed by Oklahoma, the Texas Panhandle, and Nebraska. "We try to design a publication to the current needs of the farmer-rancher in a given area," Berkely says.

As a weekly farm publication with the largest farm classified section of any farm paper in the United States, the *High Plains Journal* requires a lot of editorial support.

According to editor Galen Hubbs, this means having a full-time staff of seven editors and associate editors and up to 28 outside writers. Hubbs says that the *High Plains*' aim is to show readers how they can produce and compete in agriculture. "We help agriculture be bottom-line oriented," Hubbs claims. He says that as far as feature stories go, ". . . we must get information out to the farmer/stockman that he can use. We're people-oriented, and we have good credibility with our readers."

The publication keeps its editors out talking to farmers and stock producers in the field. "Agriculture is changing constantly, and we can constantly monitor crop conditions, market conditions, and other things as we travel," Hubbs says. "And since we travel so much, we constantly get phone calls from other people. We basically have contacts in every county to find out where we can get information."

This 37-foot wheat sculpture stands in front of the High Plains Publishers, Inc., facility in Dodge City, where it serves as a tribute to the importance of High Plains agriculture and the originality of determined people.

There is much more to be said about the High Plains than just labeling it a geographic area. For a large group of farmers and stockmen, it is a way of life that symbolizes diversified agriculture at its best—and sometimes largest. With more than 75 percent of its readers Class I farmers and 50 percent Class 1A, the emphasis is on helping the farmer help himself.

But even with the hard perspective on the bottom line, people are still the number-one priority. In talking about his readers and the *High Plains Journal* organization, Joe Berkely asserts: "A lot of organizations were built with equipment—ours was built with people."

Photo by Jeff Hetler

10

Producing and distributing goods for individuals and businesses, Kansas' industry provides employment for many of its residents.

INDUSTRY

RITCHIE CORPORATION

Since 1917, the year young Hale Ritchie laid his first brick street in Wichita, virtually all Wichita roadways, whether brick, concrete, or asphalt, have at some point a contact with Ritchie Corporation.

With roughly 550 employees and sales of $60 million, Ritchie Corporation is the largest paving and construction materials firm in Wichita, and one of the largest in Kansas. Offices in the Kansas City area, southwest Missouri, Oklahoma, and Texas extend the firm well beyond its Sedgwick County headquarters.

"We have deep roots in Kansas and a strong commitment to this state," says Hale Ritchie, co-owner of Ritchie Corporation with his cousin Tom Ritchie. The cousins are the great-great-grandsons of John Ritchie, a brigadier general in the Union Army, friend of abolitionist John Brown, and a signer of the Kansas Constitution. In 1857 he opened a rock quarry in Topeka. From this quarry came the stone for many of the capital's old buildings and the beginning of the Ritchie family's long-term commitment to the construction industry in Kansas.

His great-grandson, Hale T. Ritchie, laid brick streets as far away as Idaho and Louisiana before eventually returning to Kansas to form the paving business that ultimately grew into Wichita's Ritchie Corporation.

From paving a new highway or parking lot, to delivering the concrete or related accessories for a new building, to selling its bagged concrete and concrete repair products to consumers, Ritchie Corporation has dramatically expanded its operations within the construction industry since it first began in Wichita in 1917. With a sales growth of $50 million during the past two decades, Ritchie Corporation has mushroomed into an integrated paving and construction materials firm with eight separate but complementary operations.

Ritchie Corporation's modern in-house laboratory guarantees first quality from each of its division's products or services. Photo by Proctor T. Ritchie

Ritchie Paving, Inc., Ritchie Sand Co., Inc., Allen's Concrete, Inc., Concrete Accessories Co., Inc., Rich-Mix Products, Inc., and Rich Mix Construction Products, Inc., are some of the subsidiary corporations that make up this vertically integrated construction firm. R&A Manufacturing, a division of Ritchie Paving, maintains and repairs the large number of vehicles and equipment and even custom manufactures certain specialized equipment when needed.

Concrete Accessories' large warehouse contains the construction materials, tools, and products needed to construct or maintain anything made with portland cement concrete. Photo by Proctor T. Ritchie

This complement of equipment, paving, and construction expertise, combined with sales of raw materials, ready-mix concrete, and other construction supplies such as C-Cure and Quickrete, enables Ritchie to provide a full range of construction-related products and services for major industrial manufacturers as Boeing, Beech Aircraft, Cessna Aircraft, Koch Industries, and The Coleman Company. And it has built or repaired parking lots, streets, and highways for practically all other public and private customers in its market area.

Ritchie Paving, Inc., the largest entity within the Ritchie organization, has the ability to construct all types of pavement and is dedicated to meeting the tight schedules required by its customers with absolutely no compromises in quality. This dedication to service and quality has brought not only growth, but also recognition.

One of Ritchie Paving's construction crews at work, completing the asphalt parking area for a new apartment project. Photo by Proctor T. Ritchie

In 1987 the American Public Works Association named Ritchie Paving, Inc., as its national Contractor of the Year for projects under $2 million. Nominated by the City of Wichita, Ritchie Paving, Inc., also won the APWA's Kansas Chapter 1987 Contractor of the Year Award for projects under one million dollars.

Allen's Concrete, Inc., a ready-mix supplier and Ritchie's second-largest division, is one of the top three ready-mix concrete companies in Kansas. Recently expanded, the Wichita facilities can easily accommodate the specialized materials and increased production demanded by its customers.

In 1987 Concrete Accessories Company, Inc., which sells supplies and accessories needed in concrete construction, including reinforcement steel, industrial maintenance supplies, and specialized tools, opened its first branch office and warehouse in Lenexa to serve the greater Kansas City area.

Rich-Mix Products, Inc., manufactures and distributes ready-mix concrete in a bag, concrete repair products, and various lawn and garden items through a distribution channel of home centers, lumberyards, and building material outlets. It produces Quickrete products in Kansas City, Wichita, Oklahoma City, and Dallas.

Ritchie Corporation's nationally accredited laboratory goes a step further to guarantee quality. Its technicians field test the component materials used on job sites, evaluate their performance, and investigate or develop new materials and techniques needed in future paving or construction projects.

"It's our quality control, absolute integrity in business, and the skills and dedication of our people that separates us from our competition. The cooperation that we and our divisions share ensures greater efficiency and cost effectiveness for our customers," say Tom and Hale Ritchie.

Because the Ritchies believe in the partnership between the business community and citizens, they personally play a significant role in the Wichita community. Each of the firm's managers is encouraged to be actively involved in community affairs.

The corporation annually sponsors its own Rainbows United Golf Tournament for special children; supports Wichita's Junior Achievement; participates in Adopt-A-School, a program that links businesses with public schools; and even provides several scholarships to employees' children attending Wichita State University.

After more than 70 years in the construction business, "We're still planning for the future," says Hale, "and working to provide first-class, no-trouble service and support to our customers." Tom adds, "All of our business practices and employee relationships are governed by strict adherence to our own 11-point Corporate Code of Conduct. This has been the cornerstone of our success in the past because our customers and our employees know that they can always expect excellent performance and be treated fairly and honestly by our company. We are certain that this will become even more important in the future."

Using its modern concrete pumps, Allen's Concrete can deliver ready-mix concrete precisely where it is needed. Courtesy, Morris-Owen Associates

THE MARLEY COMPANY

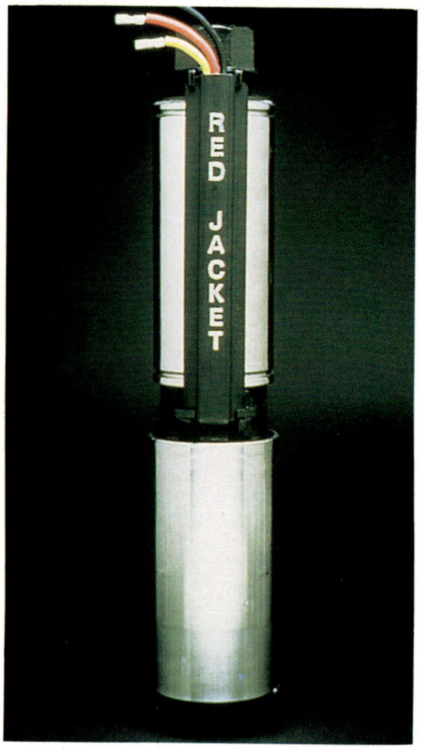

Marley Pump Company's Red Jacket brand provides pumps and accessories used in water well systems for residential, agricultural, and small municipal water-pumping systems.

Products and services from The Marley Company quietly touch everyday life in Kansas. Products of this privately held, low-profile corporation with headquarters in Mission Woods are well known, however, to operators and owners of electric power plants, municipal waterworks, gasoline stations, and irrigation systems.

Marley, with its various divisions, 12 major manufacturing facilities, annual sales of more than $600 million, and operations in all 50 states, Canada, and Europe, is a major manufacturer and supplier in the fields of cooling towers, pumps, water well drilling and repair, and heating-related equipment.

Since 1922 the company has been at home in the Kansas City area. It began as a manufacturer of large, industrial water spray nozzles used to cool water running through the condensers of electric generating stations. The firm later developed a more sophisticated form of cooling with its wide range of water cooling towers, including large, concrete hyperbolic structures that cool larger volumes of water more efficiently.

The largest manufacturer of water cooling towers in the United States and a worldwide distributor, the Marley Cooling Tower Company is the only U.S. manufacturer offering a full range of small-, medium-, and large-capacity mechanical and natural draft cooling towers.

The cooling tower subsidiary, based in Mission, also manufactures and sells evaporative condensers and closed-circuit coolers; provides tower reconstruction and repair; and serves the industrial, utility, heating, ventilating, air-conditioning, and refrigeration markets.

Until 1968 Marley only manufactured water cooling towers. Today that subsidiary represents about 20 percent of the corporation's total business. In the past 20 years The Marley Company has aggressively acquired businesses that have enabled it to diversify into water well drilling and repair, boiler manufacturing, electric resistance heating products, and the manufacture and distribution of pumps.

WATER SUPPLY SERVICES

Layne-Western Company, Inc., with headquarters in Mission Woods, is the largest water well drilling and repair company in the United States. With coast-to-coast offices and more than 500 drilling and service vehicles, the firm offers a variety of services.

Layne-Western designs, constructs, and maintains water supply and distribution systems, including the drilling of wells and installation of the screens, pumps, valves, and related equipment. These systems are generally used for industrial, municipal, and agricultural purposes.

More than one-third of the United States, and particularly Kansas, relies on groundwater. Water demands are increasing as are the concerns about contamination and lowering water tables.

With its history of innovative methods for groundwater development and expertise in hydrology and geology, Layne-Western offers environmental services, construction drilling, water-systems equipment, and related activities.

Part of Layne-Western's business involves mineral exploration drilling. Its dual-wall reverse circulation method of drilling provides uncontaminated samples, making it excellent for mineral exploration.

PUMPS

The Marley Pump Company, based in Mission, markets products under the Red Jacket and Simer brands.

Weil-McLain is the leading U.S. manufacturer of cast-iron boilers for residential and commercial buildings.

Marley Cooling Tower Company is the only U.S. manufacturer offering a full range of small-, medium-, and large-capacity mechanical and natural draft cooling towers.

Based on sales, these product lines are among the industry leaders.

Red Jacket Pumps manufactures petroleum pumps for underground gasoline storage tanks at retail gasoline stations. These specialized pumps deliver gas from underground tanks to above-ground gas dispensers. Red Jacket also manufactures pumps and accessories used in water well systems for residential, agricultural, and small municipal water-pumping systems.

Smaller, do-it-yourself pumps are manufactured by Marley Pump's Simer division.

Layne and Bowler in Memphis, Tennessee, is one of the largest U.S. manufacturers of vertical turbine pumps. The company manufactures and sells a broad range of pumps for use in municipal and industrial applications, including water wells and agricultural irrigation.

HEATING AND HEAT EXCHANGE PRODUCTS

Weil-McLain, located in Michigan City, Indiana, is the leading U.S. manufacturer of cast-iron boilers for residential and commercial operations. Its boilers use a variety of fuel and energy sources to heat water or generate steam for heating systems. Much of its business is in the replacement markets for both residential and commercial applications. Fuel efficiency, ease of installation, technical reputation, and product service availability of its products create Weil-McLain's competitive advantages.

Marley Electric Heating in Bennettsville, South Carolina, is one of the industry leaders in the manufacture of electric resistance heating products for the residential, commercial, and industrial markets.

Engineers and Fabricators Co. (EFCO) in Houston designs, manufactures, and sells shell and tube heat exchange products used in industrial processing, primarily in the chemical, paper, electric utility, and petroleum industries. EFCO also designs and manufactures feedwater heaters for electric power generation and industrial processing applications.

The Marley Company and its operating companies employ more than 4,500 people, with 800 working in Kansas, including 55 at corporate headquarters. Many of Marley's employees are highly trained specialists with expertise that together covers geology and most of the engineering disciplines—environmental, chemical, electrical, mechanical, and structural.

In 1981 Marley became a privately held company through a leveraged buy-out involving Kohlberg Kravis Roberts & Co. of New York and San Francisco. Management continues to support the research and development and customer service that helped build Marley's reputation.

Strategic acquisitions also will continue to play an important role in The Marley Company's future. The organization plans to strengthen its role in the fields where it already has specialties, such as water well drilling, electric heating, and other complementary businesses.

"We are in businesses where we are either first or second in the products we manufacture," says Robert Dineen, president and chief executive officer. "We will strive to maintain the strong customer acceptance we have enjoyed for our products."

The nation's largest water supply service company, Layne-Western also specializes in environmental, construction drilling and mineral exploration services.

BARNES & DODGE, INC.

When Roland "Skip" Phelps bought the 13-year-old Barnes & Dodge, Inc., in 1976, the sheet-metal constructor had 22 employees and a Missouri address.

Since then Phelps moved the firm to Kansas City's Kansas side and introduced state-of-the-art technology into every phase of the operation.

With $4.5 million in annual sales and roughly 50 employees, Barnes & Dodge is one of the largest sheet-metal firms in Kansas and employs the largest number of skilled sheet-metal craftsmen in the Kansas City area.

The firm includes sons Roger A. Phelps, executive vice-president/project management and estimating, and Russell D. Phelps, vice-president, who has extensive training and experience in computer applications to manufacturing.

The company's use of computer-aided drafting, computer-aided manufacturing, and its computer-controlled plasma cutting table and automatic coil line make it the area's most up-to-date sheet-metal operation.

With computers, Barnes & Dodge can easily estimate a job from working drawings and then feed those drawings through its computer-design and -manufacturing systems. That approach is efficient, faster, and more accurate. "We keep up with the new technology," says Skip Phelps, "and that's better for our customers."

Barnes & Dodge's dedication to the highest standards of quality in the design, manufacture, and installation of sheet-metal products has brought it repeat business from an impressive list of clients. The region's leading firms— Commerce Bank of Kansas City, General Motors Corp., Trans World Airlines, Marion Laboratories, Inc., Hallmark Cards, and American Telephone & Telegraph Co.—have all used Barnes & Dodge for various projects.

Firms such as Du Pont and Owens Corning Fiberglas Corp. have utilized the staff's training in pollution control, heat recovery, dust collection, and heating, ventilation, and air-conditioning.

Menorah Medical Center in Kansas City, Missouri, contracted this 11-foot-high menorah for its circle drive.

The 11-foot-high, stainless-steel menorah glimmering in the circle drive of Kansas City's Menorah Medical Center testifies to the firm's attention to detail and its skill with special projects.

On the industrial side, the firm fabricated and then erected ductwork sections 8 feet in diameter and 25 feet long at a solvent-recovery system in Leavenworth. A helicopter and an eight-man crew completed the challenging assembly in fewer than 10 hours.

With a bonding capacity of $10 million and craftsmen experienced in fine detail work, no job has been too large or too specialized for Barnes & Dodge. "We work on a team concept," explains Skip Phelps. "We're known for our quality, and we deliver on time."

Ductwork at a solvent-recovery system in Leavenworth was erected by helicopter.

FLEMING COMPANIES, INC.

Fleming is a forerunner in developing warehouses with the latest technological advances. The company operates more distribution centers using mechanized order selection systems, as shown here, than any other wholesaler. Every Fleming distribution center—whether mechanized or not—is equipped with complex computer support systems that track inventory and streamline the distribution process. Such technological innovations give Fleming the ability to be efficient and competitive—keys to profitability in a business where profit margins are slim and timing a critical factor.

Fleming Companies, Inc., the largest wholesale food distributor in the country, discovered growth and opportunities in the rapidly changing retail food business.

Its innovative approach to food distribution, attention to consumer needs, and timely acquisitions have pushed this once small food wholesaler to annual sales of more than $12 billion.

When Fleming started as a small wholesale grocery firm in Topeka in 1915, local grocers delivered a homemaker's food order to her front door. Grocers competed only with other small retailers for the family food dollar.

Large chain stores with big advertising budgets and mass-merchandising advantages gradually invaded the small grocers' domain. The independents, plagued by inefficient methods of purchasing, merchandising, and store operations, lost ground.

Under the leadership of Ned Fleming, son of company founder O.A. Fleming, the grocery wholesaler positioned itself to assist the independent food retailer with a fresh marketing approach known as the voluntary group concept. By creating a "growth partnership" between retailer and wholesaler, Fleming enabled the independent grocer to become more efficient and competitive. Independent operators remain the backbone of Fleming's retail network, accounting for two-thirds of the firm's business.

Affiliated grocers rely on Fleming's fair prices, on-time deliveries, and superb support services to help them succeed in the increasingly competitive world of retail food.

In the past five years Fleming's retail network has doubled. Today more than 5,200 affiliated retail food outlets in 36 states from New Jersey to Hawaii work with Fleming to maintain their competitive edge.

Through its 38-warehouse network with its 18.7 million square feet of computer-supported storage space, Fleming ships thousands of tons of products each day to conventional supermarkets, superstores, combinations stores, and warehouse markets operated by independent retailers and corporate chains.

An acknowledged leader in mechanized warehouse systems, Fleming continues to incorporate new technologies to achieve greater efficiency and productivity in the distribution of foods and related products. Its distribution facilities are among the industry's most modern and efficient. Its truck fleet travels millions of miles, delivering almost any item needed for a completely stocked market.

Its new distribution center in Maryland and additions to warehouse distribution centers in California and Hawaii demonstrate Fleming's commitment to improving its facilities and services.

Under the leadership of E. Dean Werries, chairman and chief executive officer, Fleming has taken a commanding market share of the wholesale food industry in the rapidly growing states of Texas, California, and Arizona, and maintains its strong presence in the Midwest, Southeast, and eastern United States.

From its headquarters in Oklahoma City, Fleming Companies, Inc., remains committed to its goal—to be the leading distributor in every market where it operates by offering its affiliated retailers the lowest-cost and highest-quality service available.

Fleming's 5,000-unit road fleet travels more than 100 million miles per year serving 5,200 stores in 36 states from New Jersey to Hawaii. More than 95 percent of the company's trucks have on-board computers that monitor vehicle and driver performance.

HILL'S PET PRODUCTS, DIVISION OF COLGATE PALMOLIVE

Hill's Science Diet and Prescription Diet products are marketed in more than 20 countries worldwide, where concerned pet owners want the best nutrition for their dogs and cats.

Hill's Pet Products of Topeka is committed to the improvement and maintenance of pet health through a balanced diet. Much more than a dog and cat food manufacturer, Hill's pioneered the concept that diseases in pets can be managed and even avoided through proper nutrition.

The business was founded in 1907 by Burton Hill as Hill's Packing Company. In 1948 the "new" Hill's Pet Products was launched. A New Jersey veterinarian, Dr. Mark L. Morris, experimented with diet to relieve symptoms of kidney failure in dogs. Morris developed a special diet that brought miraculous results and became convinced that pet health could be managed through diet. Morris made an arrangement with Burton Hill of Topeka to manufacture his special diet, later known as Canine k/d, and Hill's Prescription Diet line was born.

In 1976 Hill's was acquired by the Colgate Palmolive Company of New York and has played a key role in the success of Colgate's specialty marketing business. Spurred by the rapid growth of Hill's Pet Products, Colgate's specialty business group, including Hill's, has achieved sales of about $500 million, an increase of almost 30 percent. In turn, Colgate's substantial resources and global distribution expertise have assisted Hill's in reaching a wider audience at home and overseas. Now with more than 1,500 employees worldwide and markets in 23 countries and in all 50 states, Hill's is the undisputed world leader in specialty pet foods.

Mark Morris Associates was founded by Dr. Morris in 1962 as an independent research, development, and quality-control company. Today Dr. Mark Morris, Jr., leads this preeminent veterinary research group that enables Hill's to continue its research and new product development programs.

Ethical veterinary supply and pet supply distributors deliver Hill's products to retail customers. Hill's Prescription Diet products are dispensed exclusively through veterinary clinics. Hill's popular Science Diet line is sold through veterinary clinics, authorized pet shops, breeders, and kennels.

Science Diet provides balanced nutrition for dogs and cats in products specifically tailored to an animal's age, activity level, temperament, and breeding condition. Widely imitated, but never equaled, Science Diet is the result of extensive research that showed that excess amounts of nutrients may be just as harmful as too little.

Hill's Prescription Diet line offers almost 20 different dietary formulas that help veterinarians manage such conditions as obesity; urinary problems; kidney, liver, or heart dysfunction; allergies; and injuries. Through this product line, Hill's has remained on the cutting edge of small animal dietary management.

A professional service representative reviews Science Diet formulation information with a pet store retailer.

A veterinarian describes the proper use of a Prescription Diet product, dispensed only by veterinarians, to a client.

Zu/Preme—Hill's small line of zoo foods—is fed to bears, lions, tigers, and Max the gorilla at the World Famous Topeka Zoo.

Hill's has the largest staff of veterinarians of any pet food company in the world. These doctors work in a variety of positions throughout the company, from sales to marketing to technical support to research and development.

From the beginning Hill's special products increased awareness among veterinarians about the importance of balanced nutrition and helped create a new veterinary discipline.

Hill's develops its relationship with veterinarians while they are still in school. The firm provides its pet food to all of the 27 U.S. veterinary schools for use in their teaching hospitals, and Hill's veterinarians lecture on dietary management at every veterinary college in the United States and Canada. The company also provides thousands of dollars in scholarships and awards each year to veterinary students.

To meet growing consumer demand, Hill's has expanded its production capacity. Its latest plant in Bowling Green, Kentucky, is considered the most cost-efficient, specialty pet food-manufacturing facility in the world.

Hill's has doubled the production capacity of its original Topeka plant, which produces both dry and canned products. Hill's overseas products, chiefly canned goods, are manufactured in Topeka and shipped worldwide.

The Kansas plant supports the state's farming economy by buying Kansas grain and livestock products. A third facility in Los Angeles serves U.S. markets in the West and steadily growing markets in Japan. Additional facilities are on the drawing board.

To better support the veterinary profession, which is the cornerstone of Hill's dietary business, several acquisitions have been made in recent years. At the end of 1988 Hill's purchased Professionals' Software, Inc., of Effingham, Illinois, a leading provider of computerized veterinary practice management systems.

In 1989 it acquired the Veterinary Services Division of McKesson Corporation. The company, one of Hill's largest product distributors, has 21 locations serving veterinary practices primarily in the eastern United States.

The firm, which Hill's renamed Veterinary Companies of America, complements an acquisition by that name that Hill's made in 1987. That veterinary supply distributor serves markets in the western United States, and together these distribution companies enable Hill's to serve the veterinary profession nationwide to complement its independent distribution network.

In the 1940s Dr. Morris' research into the relationship between balanced nutrients and overall health foreshadowed a similar trend in human medicine. Today consumers are increasingly aware of the effects of poor eating habits on health and have extended this awareness to their pets.

This growing concern about health and nutrition has strengthened Hill's Pet Products' position as a premier manufacturer of quality pet foods. The company remains committed to providing superior nutrition, reducing the risk of pet disease, and promoting optimum health through dietary management.

In the background is Hill's Topeka plant on the banks of the Kansas River, where both canned and dry foods are produced for shipment nationwide and abroad.

Photo by Tom McCarthy

11

Kansas' business and professional community brings a wealth of service, ability, and insight to the area.

BUSINESS AND PROFESSIONS

KANSAS DEPARTMENT OF COMMERCE

An essential goal—economic prosperity for Kansas—drives the state's Department of Commerce. By assisting in the creation of jobs and wealth in Kansas through innovative and aggressive economic development programs, the department has accepted a dynamic challenge and responsibility.

The Kansas Department of Commerce is located across the street from the capitol in the Capitol Towers Building at 400 Southwest Eighth Street in Topeka. Its staff of 110 people and a budget of nearly $29 million makes it possible for the department to focus on five major divisions: industrial development, trade development, existing industry, travel and tourism, and community development. All work for an economically strong Kansas.

Recruiting new business to Kansas is the job of the Industrial Development Division. The domestic marketing section works with U.S.-based companies considering Kansas as a location for new business facilities. The international section recruits new business investment from international sources.

Promoting an international demand for Kansas products is the focus of the Trade Development Division. Missions to South America,

The Kansas Capitol building serves as the backdrop for the Kansas Department of Commerce and its economic development program for the state.

Asia, and Canada recently brought 16 Kansas companies more than $6 million in sales.

Trade missions to such places as the Paris Air Show, Asian Trade Mission, and Caribbean Food Show brought increased demand for Kansas products. Ten offices throughout the world distribute information about Kansas products and connect potential buyers with Kansas businesses.

Promoting and encouraging growth, diversification, and retention of business and industry in Kansas falls to the Existing Industry Division. Through its eight regional offices, the division's staff makes thousands of face-to-face and telephone contacts to extend its services and support statewide.

Increasing the number of visitors to Kansas is the focus of the Travel and Tourism Division. Its successful Linger Longer campaign has encouraged visitors alike to enjoy the state's many attractions.

Advertising in regional and national markets and promoting Kansas to the film industry are among the division's efforts to entice more people to stop and enjoy Kansas.

Creating an environment conducive to economic development is the heart of the Community Development Division. Many communities have received millions of dollars through a variety of grants for economic development and community improvement.

The new Partnership Fund assists communities in attracting businesses and extending infrastructure support. A new Rural Assistance Center has been established to help rural communities.

Kansas, Inc., Kansas Technology Enterprise Corporation, Kansas Venture Capital, Inc., and the Kansas Development Finance Authority work with the department to move Kansas' economic development forward. The Kansas Department of Commerce, together with these outside partners, spreads the word that Kansas has much to offer business and industry.

The Kansas Department of Commerce is divided into five different sectors covering every aspect of Kansas' economic potential. The Industrial Development Division works with U.S. -based companies considering Kansas as a location for new business facilities.

BUILDERS, INC.

Builders, Inc., owns Garvey Industrial Park, which covers 800,000 square feet of covered warehouse and assembly space, and is the operator of the Sedgwick County Foreign Trade Zone.

"Everything in real estate," has been the motto of Wichita's Builders, Inc., since it was formed in 1941.

Recognizing that shelter was a basic need, entrepreneur Willard Garvey established Builders as Garvey Industries' housing-related subsidiary.

In the 1950s returning G.I.s desperately needed affordable housing, and Builders prospered during this postwar building boom. The largest home builder in Wichita during this time, the firm constructed 2,400 houses and 1,800 apartments and developed 17 subdivisions. Parklane, Wichita's first major shopping center, also was developed by Builders in 1955 and continues as a thriving shopping area.

Today Builders, Inc., remains driven by a relentless commitment to the total real estate industry. Builders is engaged in commercial and residential development, construction, sales and leasing, property management, and warehousing.

Each division of Builders operates independently, but their combined expertise and strength provide tenants and investors with resources and services not found locally from a single source.

Since 1980 Builders has developed more than one million square feet of quality commercial and residential space, including 900 apartment units and 500,000 square feet of commercial and industrial properties.

GARVEY INDUSTRIAL PARK

At Garvey Industrial Park, Builders has 800,000 square feet of industrial space under one roof. Through its Garvey Public Warehouse subsidiary, the company operates a public, bonded warehouse for the small and large warehouse user. Garvey Industrial Park, has been designated Foreign Trade Zone No. 161 and offers duty-free storage of imported products awaiting distribution or final assembly for the domestic market or re-export.

BUILDERS CONSTRUCTION
For more than 30 years Builders Construction has worked hand in hand with Builders' development team as a general contractor to provide buildings on time and at a reasonable cost. Responsive to the changes in the construction industry, this division builds properties that are efficient and functional, and meet technical standards and requirements for quality.

BUILDERS DEVELOPMENT—EPIC CENTER
Epic Center, its copper roof gleaming above Wichita's skyline, is Builders' most obvious presence and its most ambitious development project to date. Begun in 1985 and completed in August 1987, this $28-million office tower with its 22 stories is the tallest building in Kansas and Wichita's premier office structure.

A Wichita landmark, the building has come to symbolize the future of business not only in Wichita but also in all of Kansas. Located in the central business district, the center is adjacent to city hall, the county courthouse, the federal courthouse, and the financial district.

Epic Center's completed site in Wichita's central business district will include two, 22-story twin office towers linked by a four-level retail galleria and atrium. Photo by Dale McCrea

In addition to its elegant interior, Epic Center offers its tenants a wide range of personal and professional services. A restaurant, hairstyling and barber shop, travel agent, tanning salon, plant showroom, and express-shipping business are among the first- and fourth-floor merchants providing essential and convenient services to the center's tenants.

Eventually Epic Center will be enlarged to a full-service, mixed-use center that will include a hotel, parking garage, and a second 22-story twin office tower, linked by a four-level retail galleria and atrium.

Epic Center is home not only to Builders, Inc., but also to prominent law offices, the Sedgwick County Law Library, accounting firms, financial services companies, and national firms such as MCI, Control Data, the Equitable Life Assurance Company, and Prudential.

MID-AMERICA WORLD TRADE CENTER

It is also home to the Mid-America World Trade Center, one of only 40 world trade centers operating in the United States. Established in 1987 as a nonprofit initiative of private business and state government, the trade center fosters the growth of international business opportunities in Kansas and the surrounding six-state mid-America region.

Epic Center is just one example of Builders' expertise in development and property management.

BUILDERS PROPERTY MANAGEMENT

Comprehensive management, whether retail, office, residential, or industrial, is a Builders trademark. A property manager for more than 40 years, Builders has grown with this rapidly expanding and demanding industry by strengthening its professional approach and marketing expertise.

Its achievements in real estate management are based upon its proven ability to meet the goal of maximizing the full income potential of a client's property. Its properties command higher rents and occupancy levels than comparable properties.

Builders currently manages 21 apartment communities with more than 3,000 apartment units, and 40 office, retail, and industrial properties. Its expansion plans include increasing Builders' regional and out-of-state management contracts.

To "find a need and fill it" has been one of the driving goals of Wichita's Garvey Industries. Finding the needs within the real estate industry and filling those special needs has pushed Builders to become one of the largest real estate companies in Kansas.

Driven by opportunity, Builders, Inc., has continued to build on its legacy of performance and commitment to the real estate industry. As it expands both within Kansas and elsewhere, the firm will continue to provide its clients with a full range of real estate services. Its proven performance ensures a strong future.

Epic Center's spacious lobby conveys a touch of elegance with its travertine-marble flooring and walls with highly polished bronze accents. Photo by Dale McCrae

GREATER TOPEKA CHAMBER OF COMMERCE

Topeka, the capital of Kansas and the hub of its northeast region, offers new facilities and expanded services for retail shopping, entertainment, health care, and educational and cultural opportunities.

This growth has enhanced the economic climate for area businesses, improved the quality of life for the city's 122,000 citizens, and provided greater opportunities for the 350,000 people in Topeka's marketing area.

Strategically located at the crossroads of I-70 and Highway 75, Topeka's market reaches 100 miles in any direction. Topeka companies brag about their central location, access to transportation, and skilled work force.

Topeka's aggressive program to expand existing businesses and to new businesses is working. Since 1983 the employment base has grown by 12,000 jobs.

Together, elected officials and community leaders have encouraged more than $500 million in investments and expansions. This push has brought new jobs at Quaker Oats, La Siesta Foods, Goodyear Tire and Rubber Co., Frito Lay, Santa Fe Railway, the U.S. Mail Processing Center, Hill's Pet Products, KPL Gas Service Co., and Blue Cross and Blue Shield of Kansas.

On the retail front, Topeka has more than doubled its retail base. An additional 1.5 million square feet of new retail space has been built, including the large and convenient West Ridge Mall and the retail development that adjoins it.

Highways and streets have been redesigned, older malls and shopping centers have undergone facelifts, and new trees, brick pathways, and benches have spruced up Topeka's downtown.

There's a can-do attitude among Topeka's citizens, elected officials, and the business and labor community. Public/private partnerships have put this attitude into action. The city and community groups have planted the many new trees seen along Topeka's busy thoroughfares.

City funds matched with private dollars made possible the renovation of the municipal auditorium into the Topeka Performing Arts Center. City funds and private investment from developer Lario Enterprises made Heartland Park Topeka the Midwest's premier motorsports racing facility. The Kansas Expocentre offers a plentiful supply of basketball games, festivals, concerts, and trade shows.

Topeka is also the home of Menninger, internationally known for its treatment and research in the field of mental illness, and Washburn University, the fourth-largest four-year university in Kansas.

The area's two lakes and almost 90 parks provide recreational opportunities for spectators and participants. Rowing, sailing, waterskiing, and the ever-popular summer ball teams lure area residents to Topeka's pleasant great outdoors.

Gage Park draws children of all ages to the 1908 Herschell Spillman carousel. This popular attraction complements the world-famous Topeka Zoo, the expansive Reinish Rose Garden, and the summer music programs in the park's amphitheater.

Without smog, traffic jams, or great distances to travel, Topeka offers an unbeatable combination—a strong business community and a superb quality of life.

Located in the center of Topeka, the Kansas Expocentre has become the hub for many community events, sporting events, rodeos, and traveling shows such as Sesame Street Live and the Ringling Brothers Circus.

A view of the downtown skyline of Topeka as seen from the southeast.

Photo by Arni Katz

12

Medical and educational institutions contribute to the quality of life of Kansas residents.

QUALITY OF LIFE

KANSAS ASSOCIATION OF COMMUNITY COLLEGES

LEFT: Burlington Northern Railroad's signal training lab at Johnson County Community College.

BELOW: An underground lunchroom is used as a classroom for Hutchinson Community College's mine safety program.

The network of 19 publicly supported Kansas community colleges is dedicated to providing students with diverse educational opportunities, at a reasonable cost and within commuting distance of their homes.

Roughly 20 years ago the colleges formed an association that brought a diverse group of schools together to work for common goals: promotion of the general student welfare, improvement of instruction, and the continued development of a quality system of public community colleges for Kansas.

Each college is governed by a local board of trustees, and all are under the general supervision of the Kansas State Board of Education. The colleges' association, however, is governed by a 76-member delegate assembly. Each college sends four representatives to the assembly—a local community college trustee, its president, a member of the faculty, and one from the student body.

From its office in Topeka, the association staff serves as a communication channel not only between the schools, but also between the schools and the Kansas Legislature. The association's executive director meets with state legislators and helps them to better understand the colleges' missions and the needs and interests of the institutions' 114 local trustees, 19 presidents, 2,000 faculty members, and more than 50,000 students.

In 1917 the Kansas Legislature authorized school districts to provide freshmen- and sophomore-level college courses. The first colleges opened two years later—Garden City in the west and Fort Scott near the Missouri border. Today 18 counties support 19 community colleges, now independent of the school districts. Together they form an educational network that reaches into nearly every nook and cranny of Kansas.

Over the years the schools' original mission to provide beginning college courses expanded, and their student bodies changed. Today the colleges offer comprehensive postsecondary education and services in addition to courses leading to several associate degrees.

The students' average age is older. Most no longer enroll in full-time studies straight out of high school. The students' average age has climbed to 31, and 75 percent attend on a part-time basis. The majority—59 percent—are women. More of today's community college students are married, possibly with children, and they are interested in upgrading job skills or retraining for a new profession.

Responding to this change, community colleges have enlarged their educational menus. They offer vocational training, remedial and developmental education, adult basic education and general equivalency diploma programs, customized training and retraining to meet business and industry needs, personal enrichment classes, career counseling and testing, and cultural programs.

All offer several associate degrees and adult basic education classes, and most offer instruction in popular programs such as emergency medical technology, office education, retail management, and instruction to become a nursing assistant.

They each may provide the basics, but the schools are as varied as the Kansas landscape, and many offer at least one program that makes a unique contribution to their communities.

Johnson County Community College, the largest of the colleges and one of the newest, primarily serves the bustling suburban area of Kansas City. The vice-president of the United States recently presented the college with the prestigious Keep America Working Award for its joint venture with Burlington

Northern Railroad. The Burlington Northern Railroad built a multimillion-dollar facility at JCC to train railroad employees from throughout the country.

Hutchinson Community College, sitting atop Kansas' salt mines, met its community's needs by offering a course in mine safety—the only course of its kind in the nation.

Labette was recently designated by the Kansas Department of Human Resources as the administrative agent for a federal grant to train dislocated railroad employees.

Highland's government procurement program helps approximately 200 businesses in Kansas' northeast corner to bid on federal contracts for supplies and services.

Aside from their most important goal—collegiate academic and vocational education for their service areas—the schools also directly contribute to the state's economy.

A Kansas City, Kansas, Community College instructor and some students discuss the latest robotic technology.

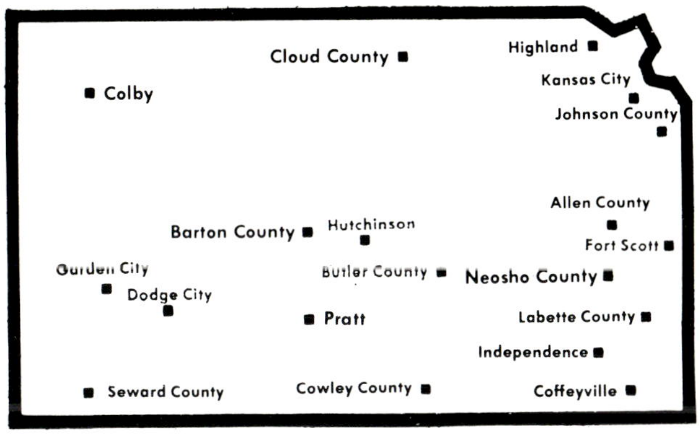

ABOVE: The black dots on this drawing of Kansas show the various statewide locations of the community colleges.

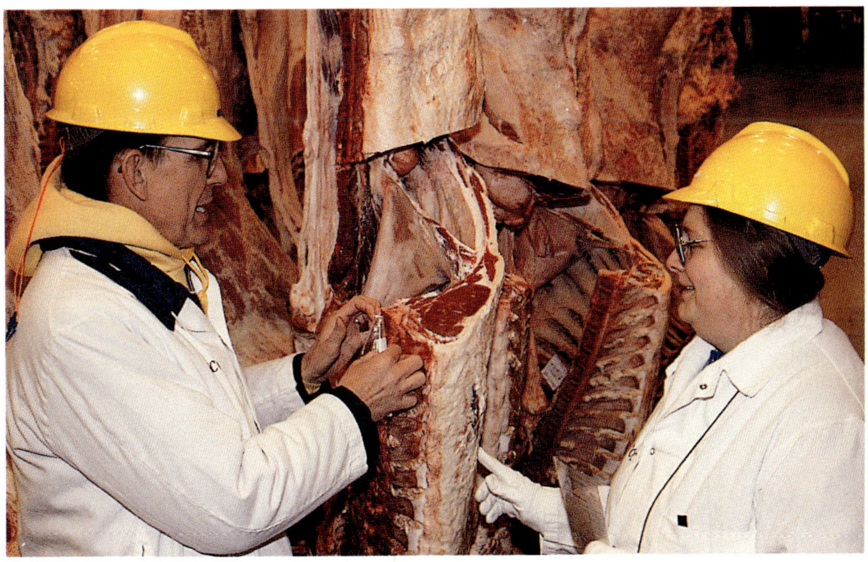

RIGHT: A Garden City Community College instructor and student determine fat characteristics inside the IBP beef plant.

Together they employ more than 3,000 Kansans in full- and part-time jobs and generate local business by increasing retail sales, utility consumption, and demand for goods and services.

Because they offer educational nuts and bolts statewide, the colleges indirectly contribute to Kansas' economic growth by educating and retraining its work force, increasing worker productivity, and helping businesses keep pace with technology.

The colleges provide educational and vocational opportunity to residents in every one of Kansas' 105 counties. In recognition of this important role, the colleges are working with the state's board of education and legislators to increase state support to community colleges to 40 percent by 1993-1994.

Currently the schools' budget totals more than $140 million and are funded at 50 percent from local tax levies, 25 percent from the state, 14 percent from tuition, 5 percent from the out-district tuition paid by counties without community colleges, and 6 percent from other sources.

Community colleges nationwide are the largest segment within higher education. A growth trend is expected to continue in Kansas, where enrollment should increase by roughly 5 percent over the next five years.

"Community colleges serve more than one need," one president says. "We take students at whatever level we find them and take them to the level they need to reach their goals."

THE WICHITA STATE UNIVERSITY

Two strong commitments—one to higher education, the other to economic growth—meld on the campus of The Wichita State University.

Wichita State, the only comprehensive urban university within the Kansas Board of Regents system of higher education, has strong economic and educational ties to the Wichita business community and Sedgwick County. This mix of city vitality and business, combined with a varied nontraditional student population, sets WSU apart from its Kansas sister schools.

Founded as Fairmount College in 1895, WSU became the first municipal university west of the Mississippi River. Today its campus, a mix of traditional buildings and modern structures, pulses with vitality, growth, and artistic appreciation. Its notable outdoor sculpture collection of 50 works by internationally known artists is accentuated by a large, vibrant Joan Miro mural.

Only 800 of WSU's 17,500 students live on its 330-acre campus. Its students are older and more established than their peers at other Kansas universities. Their average age is about 29, and many students balance jobs, families, and community activities with their studies.

The only urban university in the Kansas Board of Regents' system, The Wichita State University meets the educational, cultural, social, and commercial needs of the greater Wichita area and adjacent counties. Photo by Dan Moore

More than 70 degree programs are offered through evening classes, so it's not surprising that among Kansas' public institutions, WSU has the highest percentage of part-time students enrolled in night courses.

Almost three-quarters of WSU's students come from Sedgwick County, but every Kansas county and all 50 states are represented, and there are more than 1,000 international students from more than 70 countries. WSU also has the largest minority population of any Kansas university, and service to minorities is part of its regents' mission.

Walter J. Horn, associate professor of aerospace engineering, performs composite materials research for Wichita State's Institute for Aviation Research. A $7-million facility for this Kansas Center of Excellence was completed in 1990. Photo by Steve Ledell

Through its six degree-granting schools and colleges—business, education, engineering, fine arts, health professions, and liberal arts and sciences—WSU offers 70 undergraduate-degree programs in more than 150 areas of study and 51 graduate programs in 100 areas at the master's, specialist, and doctoral level. Included in its more than 750 full-time, part-time, and adjunct faculty are 13 distinguished professors.

WSU's programs run the gamut—music, chemistry, health professions, special education—but it is the areas of business and aviation research that dramatically tie the university to the community.

The Institute for Aviation Research is located in a new, $7-million, 74,000-square-foot facility. With resources from the College of Engineering, the Barton School of Business, and the Fairmount College of Liberal Arts and Sciences, the institute exemplifies both WSU's strong academic and technological links to the aviation industry and its commitment to the area's economy.

The School of Engineering's aero-

Wichita State's Shocker baseball team won the 1989 College World Series and the university's first NCAA national title. Courtesy, the Wichita Eagle

dynamics and composite materials laboratories complement the work performed at the institute. This aviation network gives WSU students direct contact with leading local aeronautical companies—Learjet Corp., Beech Aircraft Co., Cessna Aircraft Co., Boeing Military Airplanes—and the National Aeronautics and Space Administration (NASA).

The W. Frank Barton School of Business, the largest business school in Kansas and the first to be endowed and named, offers programs that support Kansas' business environment. The Center for Entrepreneurship, one of the earliest and the most comprehensive U.S. programs for entrepreneurs, is housed in the recently completed Devlin Hall.

WSU also serves as the program control center for the Kansas Small Business Development Centers, which provide management assistance to small businesses. WSU's Centers for Management Development and Economic Development and Business Research serve the city and state.

The first Pizza Hut, begun by WSU business majors Dan and Frank Carney in 1958, is now located on campus. The building currently houses the Association of Collegiate Entrepreneurs, a national resource for young entrepreneurs.

Wichita State is nationally known for its outdoor sculpture collection, which features the late Joan Miro's Personnages Oiseaux, *(LEFT) a marble and glass mosaic facade for the Edwin A. Ulrich Museum of Art, and Henry Moore's* Reclining Figure *(ABOVE). Photos by Paul Bowen*

WSU's $100-million Commitment to Excellence capital campaign, completed in 1989 and the first phase of a $300-million campaign, launched a building phase unparalleled in WSU's history.

In addition to Devlin Hall and the Institute for Aviation Research, campus improvements or expansions have included a Physical Plant Complex; an expansion and renovation of the Media Resources Center, the most comprehensive telecommunications center in the regents' system; the opening of the K.T. and Mary Inez Woodman Alumni Center; improvements to the baseball stadium and Tyler Field; and a science classroom and laboratory building scheduled to open in 1992. In addition, there is a 78,000-square-foot addition to Ablah Library with a dramatic sculpture plaza entrance.

WSU's regents' mission is clear: to meet the industrial, business, educational, social, and cultural needs of the greater Wichita area and to serve the citizens in the 13-county area surrounding Wichita and Sedgwick County.

A recent study shows WSU's economic impact on the area to be about $200 million annually. The university's recent improvements and its capital campaign will enable WSU to strengthen its regents' mission and deepen its support to area businesses.

The university's participation in WI/SE—the Wichita/Sedgwick County Partnership for Growth—demonstrates its commitment to the area's growth. This unique alliance of the Wichita Chamber of Commerce, city and county governments, the business community, and WSU is working to improve the area's business climate. Housed at WSU, the WI/SE Center for Technology Application matches local sources of advanced technology with the needs of businesses in the community.

Wichita State's academic programs, based on a liberal arts foundation, fulfill its mission in the delivery of programs in the visual and performing arts, engineering, business, and education, providing for a vital and mutually beneficial community/campus partnership.

WICHITA CLINIC P.A.

Wichita Clinic P.A. is located at 3311 East Murdock in Wichita.

The Wichita Clinic P.A., with more than 100 doctors serving patients in seven locations in Sedgwick and Harvey counties, is the largest multi-specialty clinic in Kansas and one of the largest in the Midwest.

The clinic handles more than 400,000 outpatient visits per year and offers patient care in more than 40 specialties and subspecialties.

The full range of medical services at the main clinic at 3311 East Murdock includes primary care, dental and psychological services, plus specialties from allergy and clinical immunology to urology. Other clinical services at the Murdock site include a cholesterol treatment center, physical therapy, a pharmacy, and stress and relaxation training. This modern clinic, completed in 1985, has more than 200 examining rooms in 130,000 square feet.

The clinic has three other Wichita locations and subsidiary offices operating under the name of The Bethel Clinic in Newton, Valley Center, and Whitewater. Specialties at the remaining satellite clinics include family practice, internal medicine, cardiology, pediatrics, obstetrics, gynecology, and dentistry.

The clinic is wholly owned by its doctors—roughly 75 percent of whom are shareholders. The clinic recruits nationwide for qualified doctors; those selected for possible membership spend two years practicing at the clinic. During this pre-association period, the professional staff evaluates the new doctors for membership.

Since its beginning in 1948, the clinic has been a leader of health care innovation. Outpatient clinics such as the Wichita Clinic are growing in popularity nationwide. The ambulatory setting offers full comprehensive care to meet patients' health care needs.

Wichita Clinic's up-to-date freestanding ambulatory surgical unit.

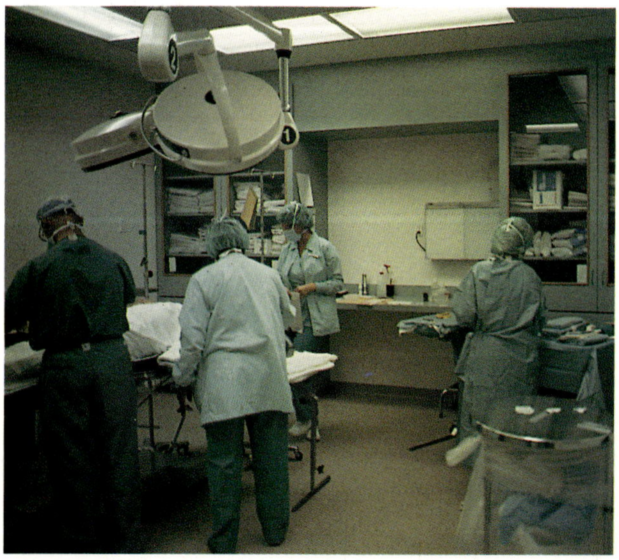

With services such as one-day surgery, full radiologic services, and outpatient chemotherapy, the Wichita Clinic provides the highest-quality, yet convenient health care.

The clinic keeps up with the latest diagnostic developments and treatments and is committed to providing the most advanced technology in outpatient practice. Magnetic resonance imaging, the technique for creating pictures of body structures or organs without using ionizing radiation, is available at the main clinic. Mammography, an X-ray exam for breast cancer, and CAT scannings also are available.

The clinic looks forward to expansion. By 1993 it will have expanded to additional sites and continue to concentrate on serving the northern counties of Oklahoma and southwest portions of Missouri.

The clinic's 10 founding physicians pioneered the area's first multi-specialty medical practice more than 40 years ago. Today this professional association of doctors of medicine, optometry, psychology, and dentistry, together with a staff of almost 500 people, meet the health care needs of Wichita and surrounding region.

The vision of those founding physicians, together with the talents, experience, and education of those who followed them, have built a medical resource respected not only in the Wichita community, but throughout Kansas.

THE UNIVERSITY OF KANSAS

Growth has become synonymous with the University of Kansas. The state's largest university heads into the 1990s with many new or expanded facilities, increased research dollars, and a stronger role than ever in the state's medical services and economic development.

KU's main campus covers the top and spills down the hillsides of Mount Oread in Lawrence. KU's presence, however, reaches beyond Lawrence to three other locations—the University of Kansas Medical Center campus in Kansas City, Kansas; the School of Medicine-Wichita; and the Regents Center, operated by KU since 1975, in Overland Park.

New construction and renovation can be found at all KU locations. With $100 million targeted for facilities, KU has more square footage under construction than at any other time in its history.

The almost $65 million in construction and renovation on the Lawrence campus includes the $13.9-million, four-story Anschutz Science Library, the $12-million Robert J. Dole Human Development Center, and the $13-million Ernst F. Lied Center for the performing arts, lectures, and symposia.

The medical center plans $28 million in building and expansions by the end of the 1990s. It has just completed a $5.5-million animal-research laboratory. Other projects include the $3-million Sutherland Institute for Facial Rehabilitation, a $3.5-million parking garage, the $2.7-million Kirmayer Fitness Center, and the $13.5-million research building. A high-technology research park north of the school's 50-acre complex may be a reality by 2020.

The Regents Center will relocate to a new $6-million facility at 127th Street and Quivira in Overland Park. The center will concentrate on providing graduate courses to the Kansas City area and will expand significantly its telecommunications capability to transmit lectures and seminars statewide.

The clinical education program at the University of Kansas School of Medicine-Wichita already has seen a $4.4-million renovation of its medical school building. Improvements continue.

The new Claude Lambe Electrophysiology Laboratory evaluates and treats heart-rhythm disturbances, and a building to house the new Wichita Center for Graduate Medical Education and refurbished space for the Family Practice Residency Clinic are planned.

Because of KU's comprehensive programs, the Kansas Board of Regents has charged the university with the responsibility to evaluate and foster the state's economic development. To achieve that mission, KU has placed a priority on the preservation and enhancement of its research and graduate programs.

KU ranks among the top 100 universities in the amount of federal research dollars it receives. Each year KU receives more than $52 million for research, and a significant amount

KU's crew rows the Kansas River.

The $14-million Anschutz Science Library was part of $65 million in major building construction under way on the KU Lawrence campus during 1989.

Strong Hall, hub of the 1,000-acre Lawrence campus.

Institute consult with owners of small businesses and assist in planning financing, market research, and product development.

Through KU's two Centers of Excellence, faculty researchers, sponsoring industries, and the state work together to further Kansas' technological development.

These university-based research centers advance basic and applied knowledge in science and technology, develop new technologies, and transfer these technologies to Kansas businesses for commercial development. These centers address the research and development needs of existing or emerging technology-based industries and offer the advantages of scale, duration, and facilities for complex research that would not be feasible for any one company to undertake.

KU is a national leader in pharmaceutical chemistry; research conducted at its Higuchi Biosciences Centers of Excellence will help to develop pharmaceutical or biotechnology businesses in Kansas. Since its start in 1983 this center has received more than $4 million from governments and industries, and has developed eight new technologies and a handful of patents.

The Center for Excellence in Computer-Aided Systems will bridge the gap between high-technology research and high-technology engineering firms. Through computer-aided analysis and design tools, the center can evaluate a design and eliminate the time-consuming process of developing prototypes, temporary tooling, and trial-and-error analysis.

In Kansas City, KU's Medical Center attracts more than $17 million per year in public and private grants

KU Medical Center pediatric cardiologist Leone Mattioli with Monica Mulls, age nine.

of those dollars work to meet Kansas' pressing needs.

Research projects from its Institute for Public Policy and Business Research include economic-impact studies, economic forecasting, and population projections for Kansas. Its scholars provide governments and business with invaluable data.

The Kansas Geological Survey studies Kansas' earth-related problems. Its staff focuses on state energy sources, mineral-industry development, environmental and engineering analysis related to land use and reclamation, and groundwater resources.

The Tertiary Oil Recovery Project studies new oil-recovery processes to increase Kansas' oil recovery, and KU's Water Resources Institute works to solve the state's water problems.

The Small Business Development Center and the Small Business

for research on such health-related issues as alcoholism, cancer, and genetics.

With an annual payroll of $110 million and 5,400 employees, KUMC is the area's fifth-largest nongovernment employer, and it is growing. Its expanded organ-transplant program; enlarged sections for kidney, liver, pancreatic, and heart treatment; and new equipment such as the gallstone lithotripter ensure the medical center will play a significant and expanding role in health care for Kansas and the region.

The University of Kansas School of Medicine-Wichita provides a community-based education program that works in cooperation with the city's private and public health care institutions and area physicians.

Each year UKSM-W provides education and training for about 100 junior and senior medical students who have completed their basic science courses at KU Medical Center in Kansas City. Instruction is offered in six departments: family and community medicine, internal medicine, obstetrics-gynecology, pediatrics, psychiatry, and surgery.

In addition to the economic and research role KU plays, the university is the academic home of almost 30,000 students. These Jayhawkers come from across the country and worldwide to enroll in one of KU's 14 academic divisions.

KU grants 30 undergraduate degrees in more than 100 fields, the master's in 90 programs, the professional degree of specialist in education, the doctor of philosophy in 50 fields, and professional doctorates in education, engineering, and musical arts. KU teaches 27 languages and offers interdisciplinary programs in East Asian, African and African-American, Soviet and East European, and Latin American studies.

Called the "wheat-belt Berkeley" and the "Harvard of the West" in college directories, KU is consistently cited as one of the "best buys" among the nation's top public universities.

Many students find KU affordable because of the Kansas University Endowment Association, which annually provides more than $8 million in scholarships, awards, prizes, and loans to students. Nearly 40,000 donors contribute almost $17 million each year for KU's benefit.

The Endowment Association, in cooperation with KU, launched the university's $177-million Campaign Kansas, the largest fund-raising effort ever undertaken by KU. The campaign seeks funds to increase scholarship support, faculty development, equipment, research, and enrichment to KU's outstanding library and museums.

KU's library system is among the top 20 public-university libraries in the nation. The Spencer Museum of Art's 21,000-piece collection is nationally known for its quality and the scope of its exhibitions. The Museum of Natural History, with almost one million specimens, is rated among the top four university natural-history museums.

In 1991 KU will celebrate its 125th year. Its anniversary festivities will include the successful completion of Campaign Kansas and the dedication of several new buildings.

For KU's centennial celebration in 1966, *Time* magazine noted that KU "has grown to a big and diverse university full in the process of self-renewal." The University of Kansas' vigorous growth continues, as does its mission to ensure the economic and educational vitality of Kansas.

The KU Lawrence campus has been called one of the most beautiful college campuses in America.

The KU Medical Center in Kansas City is known for many research and surgical specialties. A $3-million Sutherland Institute for Facial Rehabilitation is one of several medical center expansion projects.

KANSAS STATE UNIVERSITY

Anderson Hall, made of Kansas limestone, is one of the oldest buildings on campus. Now the administration building, it exemplifies KSU's picturesque architecture.

Kansas State University, situated in the rolling Flint Hills, is the state's oldest institution of higher education. Just west of the tall grass and buffalo of the Konza Prairie, Kansas State enjoys both the small-town atmosphere of Manhattan and the natural beauty of the state's landscape.

Founded in 1863 under the federal Morrill Land-Grant College Act, Kansas State is one of the nation's first land-grant schools. This strong land-grant tradition gives the school a threefold mission: to teach, research, and bring useful knowledge to citizens statewide.

The Kansas Board of Regents, recognizing the university's unique strengths, included teacher education, agricultural research, architecture, veterinary medicine, rural education, home economics, and public service in KSU's statewide mission to support rural Kansas.

Kansas State first opened its doors to 52 students—26 men and 26 women. Today more than 20,000 undergraduate and graduate students choose from more than 300 programs of study in broad areas: the liberal arts and sciences, engineering, agriculture, business administration, education, human ecology, architecture and design, and veterinary medicine.

More than 120,000 people from throughout the world and every Kansas county have come to this 668-acre campus to earn everything from undergraduate degrees through doctorates.

Many of KSU's academic programs are nationally ranked. The College of Engineering is one of only 10 U.S. colleges to be cited twice by the National Society of Professional Engineers for its outstanding professional programs. The College of Business is in the 15 percent of U.S. colleges to be accredited by the American Assembly of Collegiate Schools of Business. The accounting curriculum is ranked 13th in the nation.

At the College of Veterinary Medicine, a researcher measures this horse's blood physiology with the help of a specially designed horse treadmill.

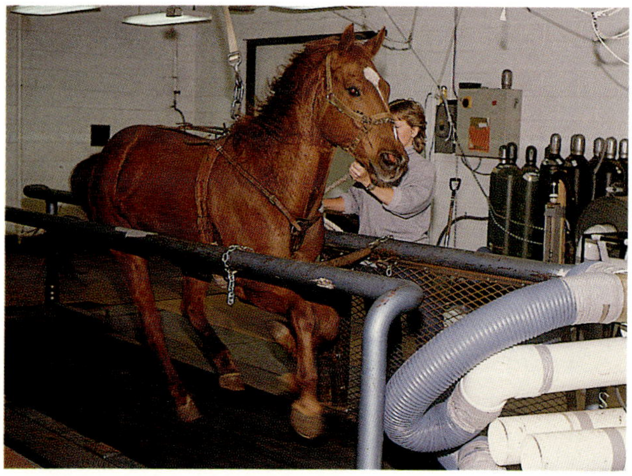

The College of Human Ecology houses the nation's fifth-ranked program in human development and family studies. KSU is also the only U.S. university offering bachelor's degrees in milling, feed, or bakery science and management as well as horticulture therapy.

In non-degree programs, thousands of Kansans in the state's 105 counties have benefited from the university-sponsored Cooperative Extension Service.

KSU's agricultural research stations, encompassing more than 12,000 acres, strengthen its rural mission. Its many agricultural-research programs and faculty are essential to Kansas' rural economy.

Its scientists conduct grain research that benefits Kansas' and the world's hungry. The university-affiliated International Grains Program promotes the marketing of wheat, corn, soybeans, sorghum, and other grains.

The Kansas Wheat Commission, the American Institute of Baking, and the U.S. Department of Agriculture's Grain Marketing Research Laboratory, all located in Manhattan, work in cooperation with Kansas State agronomists, agricultural engineers, and plant pathologists.

The Agricultural Value-Added Processing Center, created by the Kansas Legislature and associated with the university, works closely with the Kansas Technology Enterprise Corporation to boost the sale of agricultural products.

As a major research university, Kansas State's projects and expertise are diverse and dynamic. Its programs touch the present and future from farm management to space

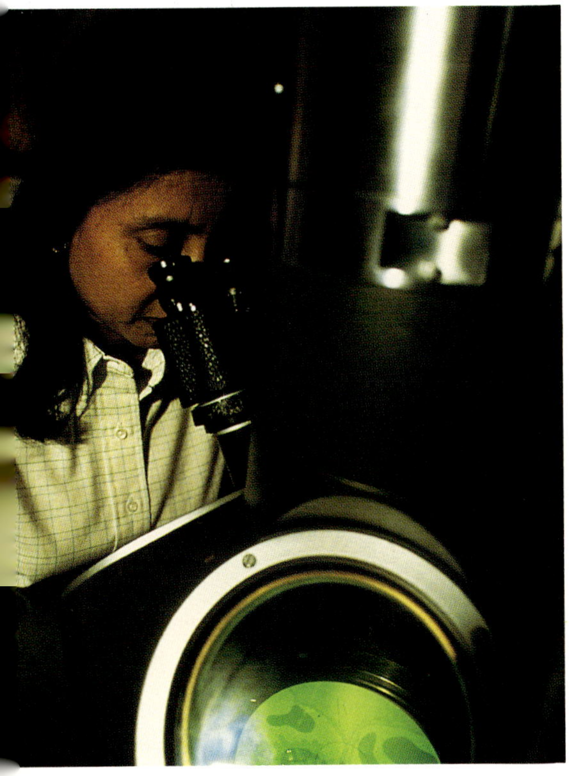

In Kansas State's department of anatomy and physiology, Asita Chatterjee uses an electron microscope to study lung damage on a horse. Courtesy, Daryl Heikes, AWAKS project

Kansas State University's Jack Higginbotham, supervisor of Kansas State's nuclear reactor, inspects the structure, located in the basement of Ward Hall. The reactor has been in operation since 1962 and is used as a teaching and research tool. Courtesy, Jim Richardson, AWAKS project

technology programs that take KSU out of the countryside and into the universe.

Because of its concerns in the areas of cancer, energy, water quality, and safe food products, Kansas State serves as headquarters for the Center for Basic Cancer Research, as a National Aeronautics and Space Administration center for the commercial development of space, and as the site of the region's nuclear-reactor research and atomic-particle accelerator.

The J.R. Macdonald Laboratory, funded in cooperation with the Kansas Legislature and the U.S. Department of Energy, is the only university accelerator facility in the nation committed solely to atomic physics.

NASA selected Kansas State's Division of Biology, in cooperation with Aerospace Engineering Sciences at the University of Colorado, to lead BioServe Space Technologies. This new center for the commercial development of space gives young biologists, plant scientists, and engineers an awareness of the opportunities in the space sciences.

The Center of Excellence for Research in Computer Controlled Automation studies computers, robotics, and artificial intelligence. The center's high-technology research will help industry expand services, manufacture new products, and increase productivity.

In fall of 1989 Kansas State, through its Kansas Regents Educational Communications Center, began transmitting classroom enrichment activities and teacher in-service programming to Kansas school districts with television satellite dishes.

This two-way, interactive teaching arrangement gives students throughout Kansas access to the best and most modern instruction available in foreign languages, science, math, writing, and special education. The program will help the problems rural schools face in recruiting teachers for these subject areas.

The U.S. Environmental Protection Agency named Kansas State one of five research centers to study hazardous substances and to educate the public and businesses about these hazards. A KSU-based consortium of seven universities will focus on problems related to mining, metal and wood-treating wastes, water, and pesticides, particularly those associated with farming.

KSU's many programs have prompted the need for expanded facilities. New buildings and renovations can be found throughout the campus. KSU's athletic teams found a new home in the Bramlage Coliseum. There is also a new chemistry/biochemistry building, and a $20-million addition to Throckmorton Hall will make KSU's plant science building the leading research facility in the world.

Adding to this construction and research momentum, KSU created The Essential Edge, its capital campaign to raise $100 million. Begun in April 1990, this major fund drive will enhance Kansas State University's programs and research that benefit Kansas and its citizens.

The prestigious Alfred M. Landon lecture series on public issues brings major figures to campus. Guest speaker former President Ronald Reagan receives a Kansas State jersey from former governor Alf Landon and U.S. Senator Nancy Kassebaum.

BETHANY MEDICAL CENTER

Bethany Medical Center is a modern medical complex with 426 licensed beds, 300 physicians, 400 nurses, and 1,000 support personnel that provide full-service health care.

Bethany Medical Center in Kansas City first began meeting the area's health care needs in 1892.

Today this modern medical complex, with 426 licensed beds, 300 physicians, 400 nurses, and 1,000 support personnel, provides full-service inpatient, outpatient, and educational health care services to the metropolitan area and Midwest region.

Near the turn of the century, immigrants seeking jobs at the packinghouses helped a young Kansas City, Kansas, to grow. Increased industrial accidents and frequent outbreaks of influenza created an unprecedented need for health care.

Six citizens met this need with a hospital. One of them even sold her diamond ring to help raise money to open the 15-bed Bethany Hospital.

Growing community need, along with strong community support, made a large, new hospital possible in 1916. This early building remains part of today's complex, composed of several wings and much-expanded services.

Now, with more than 73,000 patients per year, Bethany Medical Center treats about 30,000 people in its emergency rooms, registers almost 20,000 outpatients, and delivers almost 1,000 babies per year. Gross revenues from patients exceeded $75 million in 1988. Operating costs, contractual cost discounts, and care provided to the needy bring Bethany's yearly revenue after expenses to about $2.5 million.

As a broad-service, community-based, nongovernmental medical center, Bethany's mission is to provide as comprehensive a range of high-quality health services as possible to Wyandotte County and eastern Kansas and to seek additional service opportunities in its region. Bethany Medical Center has shown by its medical achievements and innovative services that it has followed that mission.

The Hartford Unit, the world's first coronary intensive care unit, opened at Bethany in 1962 under the vision of Dr. Hughes Day. He hoped that isolated and increased supervision of patients susceptible to cardiac arrest would lower the mortality rate of heart attack patients. Within five years Day's intensive-care unit reduced the death rate from 40 percent to 18 percent.

Day also chose the alert call "code blue" as a hospital-wide signal that a patient was in cardiac distress and required immediate life-saving procedures. Today "code blue" is known to health care professionals worldwide.

In 1968 Bethany opened Kansas' first continuing care unit, the bare beginnings of what would become its rehabilitation unit. The unit serves as a transition between a patient's acute hospital stay and a gradual preparation to return home.

Other innovative treatment approaches include Bethany's Wound Care Center. Affiliated with CuraTech, Inc., the center provides specialized care for chronic wounds unresponsive to standard care. Unhealed wounds in diabetics can be particularly alarming. Through the center's comprehensive therapy, amputations have been drastically reduced. The program provides state-of-the-art wound evaluation, advanced techniques to stimulate healing, and frequent follow-up outpatient care at a lower total cost than standard therapy.

Bethany's Chemical Dependency Program, one of the first inpatient programs in the region, offers hope and help to drug and alcohol dependents and their families. A free preadmission evaluation assesses the extent of an individual's dependency. The specially trained treat-

Recognized as a broad-service, community-based, nongovernmental medical center, Bethany Medical Center provides a comprehensive range of high-quality health services to Wyandotte County and eastern Kansas.

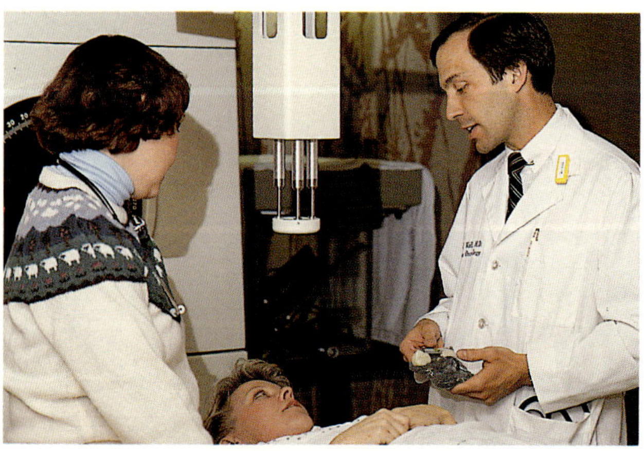

ment team of nurses, consulting physicians, and counselor technicians compassionately manage withdrawal symptoms and offer the patient encouragement, support, education, and relapse prevention.

The patient's family and concerned friends are encouraged to participate in the free Family Recovery Program. Lectures and group, individual, family, and after-care counseling services help to build a new life and support the patient's ongoing recovery.

Bethany's Voice Clinic is an innovative service devoted exclusively to the development of voice perfection.

ABOVE: Expertise combined with a genuine attitude is a trademark at Bethany. This attitude is reflected in Bethany's commitment to the primary nursing philosophy, where each nurse is assigned a patient and continues with that patient throughout his or her hospital stay. Courtesy, Mac Carver Photography

RIGHT: By actually performing or simulating normal work activities, Bethany's Work Capacity Evaluation and Work Hardening program helps patients return to their jobs as productive employees. Through this and other innovative programs, Bethany demonstrates its continual awareness of the changing needs in health care and the community. Courtesy, Mac Carver Photography

The clinic serves a variety of clients, from those who professionally rely upon a clear, effective speaking voice to those who have lost their voice and need rehabilitation.

Bethany's 24-Hour Outpatient Unit provides a safe, cost-effective alternative to patients who need extra care before or after various exams, but do not need to be hospitalized. The unit allows patients to be observed after diagnostic testing, to receive special help in preparing for some exams and treatment, or to be monitored to determine the severity of an illness.

The Day Surgery Program offers advanced family health care in a fully equipped outpatient surgical facility. Breast biopsies, tonsillectomies,

Since 1892 Bethany Medical Center has been meeting the needs of the community it serves, offering compassionate care, innovative programs, and advanced technology. Today the hospital continues its tradition as an innovative leader in the health care industry. Courtesy, Mac Carver Photography

vasectomies, cataract extractions, and even cosmetic and plastic surgeries are performed without overnight hospital stays. Preoperative education and postoperative telephone calls ensure a smooth recovery.

The Diabetes Education Program helps diabetics learn to meet the challenges of diabetes and lead healthy, independent lives. This 15-hour program enables patients to play a part in designing and maintaining their treatment plans and to learn to assess, understand, and manage their disease and prevent long-term complications.

The center's maternity options include the one-room concept, where labor, delivery, and recovery occur in one place. Families can select convenient and economical one-day maternity care or longer, more traditional maternity stays.

From cardiac care to childbirth, cancer treatment to home-health services, health screenings to education, Bethany is committed to well-rounded patient care that meets the needs of the Kansas City area.

ST. FRANCIS HOSPITAL AND MEDICAL CENTER

Topeka's St. Francis Hospital and Medical Center is a voluntary, non-profit, 378-bed, acute care facility. One of the eight hospitals in the Sisters of Charity of Leavenworth Health Services System, this ultra-modern facility provides comprehensive health care for a population base of almost 600,000 people.

With more than 1,600 employees, St. Francis is one of the community's largest employers. The more than 300 physicians on the medical staff of St. Francis care for almost 120,000 inpatients and outpatients each year.

St. Francis offers a wide range of medical and surgical services, but it is especially known for its cancer, cardiology, and rehabilitation programs and for its NewLife Center, providing family-centered maternity care.

The Capital Region Radiation Oncology Center serves the people of northeast Kansas as the principal center for radiation treatment of cancer. Recognized as one of the state's premier facilities, the center now treats 90 to 120 patients each day. Certified as a comprehensive cancer center, St. Francis is committed to the prevention, early detection, and treatment of cancer. This uniquely compassionate and technically competent oncology center is rapidly gaining a reputation as one of the finest community cancer centers in the country.

It offers advanced procedures in treatment and diagnosis, state-of-the-art technology and equipment, community screenings and education, and a full range of support services for patients and their families.

The radiation therapy center offers a free transportation service to clients in several communities west, north, and southeast of Topeka. Available to all patients regardless of financial need, the van is a boon to cancer patients who come to the center five times per week for several weeks.

St. Francis also is a regional leader at the technological forefront of cardiac care. Its cardiology programs use a variety of diagnostic tools and procedures, including nuclear scans, stress testing, echocardiograms, electrophysiology studies, and cardiac catheterizations.

The cardiac team performs advanced procedures such as defibrillator implantation, open-heart surgery, valvuloplasty, and angioplasty. Lasers are available to treat peripheral vascular diseases.

From its 24-hour monitoring for the acutely ill, to its telemetry unit for the more stable heart patient, to its Change of Heart cardiac rehabili-

St. Francis Hospital and Medical Center has served the medical needs of northeast Kansas for more than 75 years with compassion and a special concern for the poor, the sick, and the helpless. Photo by Larry Schwarm

The spirit of St. Francis is evident throughout the hospital—in its staff and its patients—from the miracle of new life to the renewal of life following a heart attack. Photo by Nathan Ham

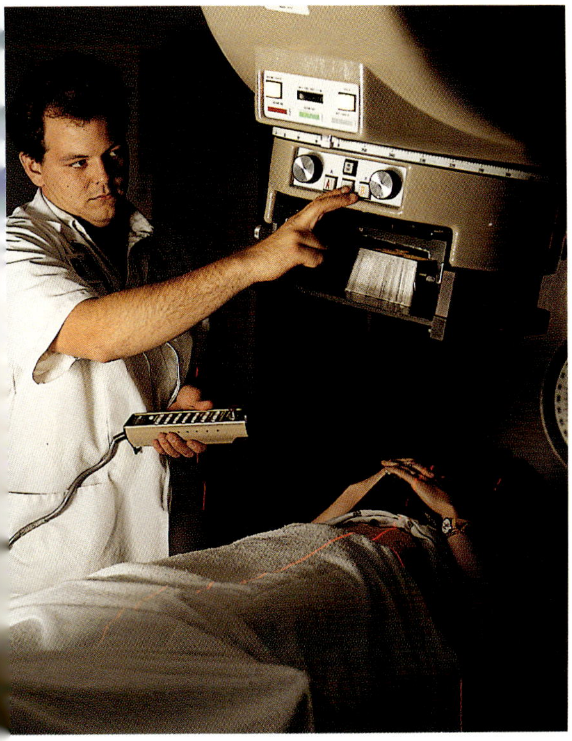

A certified comprehensive cancer center, St. Francis is committed to the prevention, early detection, and treatment of cancer. Its Capital Region Radiation Oncology Center serves as a premier facility for radiation treatment of cancer patients. Photo by Nathan Ham

tation exercise program, St. Francis provides comprehensive cardiac care.

The hospital's Rehabilitation Center was established in 1985 as northeast Kansas' first comprehensive rehabilitation unit. This 28-bed center includes Easy Street, a real-life environment where patients face the real and sometimes frightening barriers of everyday living.

With its life-size replicas of Topeka businesses and community settings, Easy Street builds confidence in patients who must adapt to wheelchairs, walkers, and other movement aids. Patients can practice maneuvering a wheelchair through a turnstile, using a department store dressing room, boarding a bus with a walker, and a number of similar daily living activities.

At the center, specialty teams care for patients with strokes, head and spinal cord injuries, amputations, and neuromuscular diseases.

At St. Francis, birth truly is a family affair. The hospital's NewLife Center emphasizes family involvement, privacy, parental control and choices, and well-baby care. Expanded visiting hours ensure that grandparents and siblings can easily visit mother and baby at any time.

Patients can choose the option of birthing in a labor/delivery/recovery/postpartum room that lets mothers and their families stay in one comfortable room from admission to dismissal. Shared Care rooms with queen-size beds accommodate the stay of father, baby, and mother. Fashionable wall coverings, floral fabrics, carpeted hallways, mahogany furnishings, even whirlpool baths make the NewLife Center a homey and comfortable place for the entire family.

St. Francis' Partners in Health offers local businesses and industries access to a centrally coordinated occupational health program for their employees. A work hardening program helps individuals return to work following an injury.

The hospital also offers more specialized services and programs. The Kansas Eye Institute and Low Vision Clinic serve patients who need treatment for eye diseases or who have severe visual handicaps but can see enough to use specialized equipment. The Chemical Dependency Treatment Services offers comprehensive treatment for persons with drug or alcohol dependencies and their families. The caring, low-cost, professional help includes intensive day or evening outpatient therapy and a flexible-stay inpatient treatment.

The Special Needs Home Health Care program sends specially trained professionals and sophisticated medical equipment to patients in their homes. The recently developed Sleep Disorders Center provides evaluation, diagnosis, and treatment for disorders such as sleep apnea, snoring, narcolepsy, nightmares, bed wetting, and sleep/talking.

In 1988 the Sisters of Charity of Leavenworth Health Services Corporation and St. Francis Hospital and Medical Center opened the Marian Clinic. The clinic provides primary medical care to individuals and families who cannot afford basic health care services.

A cooperative effort between the Sisters, hospital, and community, the clinic is an active example of St. Francis' ongoing dedication to provide health care regardless of a patient's ability to pay. Each year the hospital donates almost $2 million in free health care to the area's medically indigent.

Since its founding in 1909, St. Francis Hospital and Medical Center has met the needs of the Topeka community. Dedicated to the Christian ethic that concern for others should rise above self-interest, it remains committed to its mission to provide quality, personalized patient care to all.

Tucked away in a corner of the Rehabilitation Center is Easy Street, a series of life-size replicas of places and settings in the community where patients learn and practice everyday living skills as they progress toward greater independence. Photo by Aileen Anderson

KANSAS COLLEGE OF TECHNOLOGY

Kansas College of Technology, located in Salina's Schilling Industrial Complex, is the only Kansas school singularly devoted to technology programs. The college is the only two-year school in the Kansas Board of Regents system. Its mission is to provide a technology curriculum that will benefit not only students but also the state's businesses and industries.

Founded in 1965, the college offers 13 engineering technology programs through six departments: aeronautical, computer science, electronic engineering, industrial engineering, civil engineering, and mechanical engineering technologies.

The college emphasizes a combination of theoretical and practical training, and students receive a blend of laboratory and classroom experiences. Graduates work with engineers and scientists in business, industry, government, and aviation to provide valuable services, skills, and products.

Many of the college's programs are unique to U.S. technological schools. Its aeronautical department, which attracts 23 percent of the school's enrollment, is particularly strong and reflects the growth in Kansas' aviation economy.

The Professional Pilot Flight School is the college's fastest-growing program, and its aviation maintenance programs have experienced similar growth.

In 1990 the college will open its international pilot training center. The program will be run in conjunction with Bricom International and Bristow Helicopters of London and 288 international pilots will train in Salina over a three-year period. The international pilot training program is the first program that the British Civil Aviation Authority has allowed outside the United Kingdom.

The institution also has formed a partnership with the Kansas National Guard to train its personnel in computer skills. This training will be used to standardize National Guard offices throughout Kansas. The college's mobile computer laboratory provides businesses with on-site computer training for their workers, who use the laboratory IBM-compatible computers and current software.

Extensive laboratory work in all technologies prepares graduates for immediate employment. The college placement rate is 92 percent.

Kansas College of Technology has experienced record growth, with enrollments of about 700 students each semester. Its students are a mix of recent high school graduates and young adults returning to college, changing careers, or just beginning their college education. The average age of its full- and part-time students is 29 years.

Its rigorous programs require that students have strong backgrounds in mathematics, communications, and computer literacy. The college offers evening and weekend degree programs, and during its 24 years has graduated more than 1,500 students—70 percent of whom have remained in Kansas.

Kansas College of Technology is fully accredited by the North Central Association, and its aeronautical programs are certified by the Federal Aviation Administration. Its programs in civil, computer, electronic, and mechanical engineering technologies are accredited by the Technology Accreditation Commission of the Accreditation Board for Engineering and Technology.

The college's training center for international pilots will be operational in July 1990.

Photo by Jeff Hetler

Photo by Arni Katz

13

Kansas' retail establishments, service industries, and products are enjoyed by residents and visitors.

MARKETPLACE

SHEPLERS, WESTERN WEAR

Sheplers, Inc., of Wichita, with a retail western-wear inventory that ranks second to none in the world, welcomes the 1990s with plans for robust expansion and a strong commitment to its steadfast customers. With 14 stores in Kansas, Missouri, Nevada, Colorado, Oklahoma, and Texas, Sheplers is considering expansion into Arizona, New Mexico, and Utah, within the next few years.

Jeans and boots by the thousands, western shirts, leathers, belt buckles, hats, Indian jewelry, western outerwear, sport coats, fringed dresses, and accessories fill its flagship store on Wichita's west side. In 60,000 square feet of retail space—slightly larger than a football field—Sheplers offers the well-known brands in western clothing—Wrangler, Levi's, Stetson, Lucchese, Justin, Dan Post, Resistol, and Panhandle Slim.

Its clothing comes in all sizes, for everyone from tiny wranglers to large-size adults. Offering on-site alterations while customers wait, Sheplers boasts it has never lost a satisfied customer.

"People come to Sheplers because we have the best assortment of western clothing and accessories that money can buy," explains Lou Cohen, Sheplers' president and chief executive officer. "We work overtime to keep our customers and take pride in our service."

Sheplers' famous sign and pylons outside of the Wichita store.

Its service includes free hat shaping, regardless of where the hat was purchased, and a complete-satisfaction guarantee, based on the old-fashioned handshake policy of Harry Shepler.

Wichita still had an Old West feel when Harry Shepler bought the 47-year-old Gibson Harness Co. in 1946. Over the years the inventory at Harry Shepler's Saddlery Co. expanded to include hats, leather goods, and western shirts, and the store moved to the present location.

Retailer Robert Dry bought the company in 1968 and built a new store with high-beamed ceilings and southwestern decor. He added jeans, boots, and ladies' apparel; published the first Sheplers catalog; opened a store in Oklahoma City; and developed plans for others in Denver and Dallas/Fort Worth. In 1976 Dry sold Sheplers for $22 million to W.R. Grace, a New York-based, multinational conglomerate.

The urban cowboy craze of the late 1970s brought excitement and a heady optimism to Sheplers. It added trendier western wear to its inventory and opened new stores to satisfy the rush for western design. The craze evaporated, and Sheplers' future momentarily looked shaky.

Sheplers offers its customers jeans and boots by the thousands, all kinds of western wear, and, for those authentic cowboys, saddles and spurs.

When Grace announced it wanted to sell its retail operations to concentrate on other businesses, Sheplers' managers knew they wanted to buy the eight-store western chain and catalog operation from W.R. Grace. The management group included Cohen; John Mosley, senior vice-president and chief financial officer; Mike Anop, senior vice-president/stores and operations; Greg McDuffie, senior vice-president/merchandising; John Wilcox, vice-president/sales promotion; and Stan Gall, vice-president/catalog.

The group was confident that aggressive management and marketing and a rededication to the tried-and-true western customer could turn the firm around. The group's main partner in the buy-out, Kansas Public Employees Retirement Fund System, shared the group's optimism

and had confidence in its entrepreneurial instincts. It purchased 49 percent of Sheplers' common stock and all of its preferred stock and loaned the company more than $9 million, bringing its debt and equity financing investment to $11.088 million.

In December 1986, after yearlong negotiations, the group completed the leveraged buy-out. It was in excess of $12 million. Once again Sheplers was a Kansas-owned and -operated company. The buy-out ensured the firm would remain in Wichita. On July 28, 1989, Sheplers retired its debt with the Kansas Public Employees Retirement System (KPERS). Sheplers employees made this happen in the 2.5 years, or half of the original projected time. KPERS members benefited with a substantial profit of more than $16 million. "Being ahead of projections in both growth and profits allowed this early action to happen," stated Lou Cohen.

Today yearly payroll for its Kansas associates totals $5 million. Industry estimates place Sheplers' annual sales at more than $100 million, with roughly two-thirds coming from its retail stores and one-third from its catalog division.

In 1988 Sheplers mailed 14 million catalogs throughout the United States, Canada, Europe, and Japan. It advertises the largest and finest selection of boots available by mail, and its expansion plans include even greater catalog exposure.

Tiny wranglers to large-size adults can find the best selection of well-known brands in western clothing at Sheplers. Wrangler, Levi's, Stetson, Tony Lama, Dan Post, and Resistol are just some of the names that have given Sheplers its reputation for quality western wear and accessories.

Sheplers will open four to six new stores every year between 1989 and 1994. Its new Boots Plus concept of a 3,000- to 3,500-square-foot store specializing in all brands of boots, with some hats, jewelry, and accessories will be part of this expansion. The first Boots Plus store opened in July 1988 in Independence, Missouri, followed that September by another in Lenexa's Oak Park Commons, just outside Kansas City.

Having comfortably turned the business around, the new management group clearly enjoys what it is doing. "We're in business to make friends and have fun," says John Wilcox.

Sheplers intends to stand firm on remaining a western-wear outfitter for customers who wear western clothing as a way of life. "Sheplers has been serving the needs of the American West since 1946," relates Cohen. "It began as a country store dedicated to the folks who built America from the ground up. We won't change unless our customers want us to."

A motto hangs in Wilcox' office, and it is signed by Ol' Shep, Sheplers' mascot, who looks like a crusty old prospector. The sign reads: "If it ain't western, if it ain't denim, if it ain't a jean or jean related, it probably doesn't belong at Sheplers."

Pictured here is a partial overview of Sheplers' flagship store in Wichita. With 60,000 square feet of retail space, it is slightly larger than a football field.

VOLUME SHOE CORPORATION

The corporate headquarters of Volume Shoe Corporation is located in Topeka, where the firm commenced its operations.

Volume Shoe Corporation, the nation's largest retail chain of self-service family shoe stores, has always called Topeka its corporate home.

Founders Louis Pozez and his cousin Shaol Pozez opened their first shoe store in Topeka in 1956. Their fresh idea of self-service and a commitment to low prices distinguished Volume Shoe from its competitors.

Today the firm's familiar trade name, Payless ShoeSource, reminds customers of moderately priced shoes for the entire family. As the Payless television commercials ask, "You could pay more, but why?"

In November 1979 the cousins sold Volume Shoe to the May Department Stores Company of St. Louis. Today May is one of the nation's largest retailing firms, operating department and specialty stores nationwide.

By the time Volume became a division of May, the cousins had expanded from one Kansas store to 757 nationwide and employed 3,500 people.

The company now employs nearly 15,000 associates in more than 2,700 stores in 44 states and the District of Columbia. In Kansas, nearly 1,500 associates work in 44 Payless ShoeSource stores, the corporate office, and the distribution center.

Volume's five-year plan to open at least 200 new stores each year through 1993 will maintain the phenomenal growth that has pushed its annual sales well over one billion dollars in less than 34 years of business. "We sell shoes, that's all we do," says R.D. Stutzman, executive vice-president/retail operations.

There are shoes everywhere in Volume's expansive corporate headquarters—on desks, shelves, and tables or in the model store displays. Alone or in pairs, in basic tones or bright colors, shoes star in the pictures, posters, and sample Payless ShoeSource ads found on the walls.

An electronic sign in the associates' work entrance keeps a running total of the week's sales. The steadily flashing numbers often show weekly figures in the hundreds of thousands of pairs sold. There is no doubt that for everything from sturdy work boots to colorful high heels to toddler sneakers, Volume Shoe sells footwear by the millions each year.

Most of Volume's shoes pass through its large distribution center just north of Topeka. Good location is only one of the reasons the company plans to stay there. "Kansas' central location, good transportation, and its strong employee work ethic can only benefit a distribution business such as ours," says Dale W. Hilpert, Volume's chairman and chief executive officer. Hilpert joined the firm in 1980 and became its chairman two years later.

Expansion will continue to play a big role in Volume's future. In recent years the first Payless ShoeSource stores opened in North and South Carolina and New York State. Texas and California, with their growing populations, will continue as strong market areas.

The pressures that come with fast-paced expansion and sales, however, will not deter Volume Shoe Corporation from its original mission—to offer family footwear at affordable prices.

Volume Shoe Corporation operates more than 2,700 Payless ShoeSource stores in 44 states.

DILLON STORES

For more than 70 years Dillon Stores, a Kansas-based retail grocery chain with 61 stores in 28 communities, has prided itself on innovation and service.

In 1913 J.S. Dillon opened his first cash food market in Hutchinson. Charge accounts were the custom, so Dillon made his unusual cash-only policy more palatable by offering savings for paying cash. Four generations of Dillons have continued the founder's policy to give customers the best service and a full dollar's worth of merchandise for every dollar spent.

Always looking for better ways to sell groceries, Dillon Stores was the first in the country to use fluorescent lighting, and among the first to use refrigerated grocery cases and trucks, and self-service shopping. Public rest rooms, air conditioning, off-street customer parking, and generic-brand foods were all fresh ideas when Dillon introduced them to Kansas.

Its early stores advertised "Complete Food Service," a motto that remains true today. Dillon continues to add products and conveniences that give shoppers what they need. Pharmacies, salad bars, delicatessens, seafood shoppes, bakeries, flowers, a post office, and video tape rentals are all under one roof, and the roof keeps getting larger. The stores have grown from 20,000 square feet in the 1940s to today's 60,000-square-foot super-stores.

Dillon's special-order service and ethnic and gourmet food aisles let every shopper satisfy that special taste, whether it is for octopus or a regional beverage.

Dillon Stores is the cornerstone division of the diversified Dillon Companies, now owned by The Kroger Company of Cincinnati. The division employs more than 6,000 Kansans and generates a yearly payroll of more than $85 million.

An example of one of Dillon's newest stores, in Wichita. Though the store exteriors take on a number of different architectural styles, the interior ambience is unmistakably Dillon's in every store. Warm colors, extra-wide aisles, and excellent lighting are familiar trademarks denoting the look and feel of a Dillon store.

A supporter of Kansas farmers and ranchers, Dillon helped the Kansas State Board of Agriculture develop the "From the Land of Kansas" program, which identifies and promotes Kansas products.

Dillon carries more than 90 of the items licensed to display the logo of a sunflower atop the state outline. When the state's 1988 Celebrate Kansas Food promotion began, Dillon was its largest retail supporter.

Dillon buys almost 6 million dozen eggs, 13 million gallons of raw milk, and 22 million pounds of dressed-weight beef per year from Kansas producers. Local flour mills grind more than 13 million pounds of Kansas wheat for Dillon's private-label breads. Its Sunnywheat Bread, made exclusively with Kansas-produced sunflower seeds, flour, honey, salt, wheat, oats, soybean oil, and milk, is the official state bread by senate proclamation.

"We're a Kansas company and we depend on the Kansas economy for our success," says Ken Keefer, director of advertising and public relations for Dillon Stores.

Innovation, service, and stores with an unmistakable ambience and convenience will continue to be the chain's trademark as the next generation of Dillon Stores moves into the 1990s.

Cake decorating takes place in-store; from simple birthday cakes to multilayered wedding cakes, Dillon Stores answer the needs of today's customer. Specially trained decorators can custom design virtually any type of cake. This is just one more example of Dillon's commitment to the one-stop shopping concept. Courtesy, Rogowski Photography, The Kroger Company

THE BRENNCO COMPANIES

The Brennco Companies, at 7701 College Boulevard in Overland Park, reflect the professional passions—health insurance and travel—of their founder and chief executive officer, James C. Brenneman.

Insurance came first for Brenneman, who worked for Security Benefit Life Insurance Company in Topeka while studying for a degree in business administration at Washburn University, from which he graduated in 1965. He did not get into the travel business until 1983, several years after he had launched the first of his insurance companies.

The Brennco Companies occupy more than 20,000 square feet of space on both levels of this graceful building on College Boulevard in Overland Park. Photo by Jeff Locklear

James C. Brenneman, president of The Brennco Companies, is personally involved in the management of his enterprises and sets the tone for the corporation with his infectious enthusiasm for the task at hand. Photo by Jeff Locklear

Insurance operations housed within the Brennco Building include Brennco Benefit Administrators, Inc., a third-party health insurance administrator; Brennco Insurance Marketing, Inc.; and Brennco Risk Management, Inc. The travel companies are Brennco Travel, Inc., a full-service agency; Cruises by Brennco; Tours by Brennco; and Club Costa Travel Club.

Brennco companies not directly involved in either insurance or travel are National Benefit Association, Brennco Association Management, Ltd., and Brennco/Burns Marketing, Inc. Brenneman, whose typical work day begins at 6:30 a.m. and extends far into the evening, is heavily involved in the management of each of the enterprises.

Brennco Benefit Administrators, Inc., the flagship company, got its start in 1978 when Brenneman set up a general insurance agency called BenMarCo that specialized in group life, disability, and medical insurance. In the beginning the benefit programs sold by BenMarCo were administered by a sister company, Continental Administrative Services, Inc. (CASI).

But in 1981, to meet a growing demand for administrative services, Brenneman organized Administrative Concepts, Inc., which became Brennco Administrators in the spring of 1988.

Today Brennco administers and provides claims-payment services for more than 30,000 people insured under employer-group or individual medical plans sponsored by the National Benefit Association. Brennco has earned a national reputation for the high quality, efficiency, and speed of its service, as well as for its innovative approach.

Brennco Insurance Marketing develops marketing materials, recruits agents to sell the insurance plans in the Brennco portfolio, and negotiates with insurance underwriters for major medical or supplemental insurance plans that would enhance the product line. BIM markets its products through a national network of approximately 150 distributors—all large, general agencies—who have, collectively, about 2,000 active agents. BIM also functions as a distributor, working directly with agents who have no agreement with an independent distributor.

Brennco Risk Management provides a variety of services in the property and casualty insurance area, including risk-management consultation, claims management, claims audits and information systems, safety and control, and other support services for insured and self-insured plans. Services include insurance-program review as well as the formulation, implementation, and monitoring of alternative risk-management programs.

Brennco Travel, acquired in 1983, concentrated on arranging business travel for corporate accounts in the

Jim Brenneman enjoys a light moment with three Brennco executives—Annette Wickliffe, vice-president/personnel and licensing; Chet Wisniewski, Jr., executive vice-president and director of operations; and Steve Sachs, vice-president and treasurer. Wickliffe was one of the first Brennco employees, beginning more than 10 years ago as a secretary. Photo by Jeff Locklear

early years of its existence. Since 1986, when Brennco became the travel agency of record for Club Costa Travel Club, another Brennco company, the agency has given equal emphasis to leisure and vacation travel, which now accounts for approximately half of total revenue. Tours by Brennco recently began developing packaged tours to domestic and international destinations that it will begin marketing starting with the 1990 vacation season.

Cruises by Brennco, a cruise-only agency, was launched in 1988 and quickly became a national force because of its low prices, number of prime sailing dates available, and extra benefits and services, such as free trip-cancellation insurance. Cruises by Brennco maintains a list of more than 1,000 sailing dates and specializes in heavily discounted special-interest cruises.

Club Costa Travel Club, with a membership approaching 30,000 people, offers savings on air fare, cruises, tours, resort condominiums, domestic and international hotels, and rental cars. The savings offered by the club on resort condos and international hotels are especially attractive and have been favorably cited on several occasions by a leading consumer travel letter. Members who purchase travel arrangements receive savings certificates that may be used to defray the cost of future travel. Members also receive a members-only magazine and newsletter, each published quarterly. A family membership, which includes unmarried children under age 23 not living at home, costs $49 per year.

Brennco/Burns Marketing develops and markets noninsurance ancillary products such as eye wear, hearing aids, medical laboratory testing, and legal assistance at discounted prices.

The National Benefit Association provides benefits for its members designed to help them purchase products and services for less than they would normally pay. Benefits available for the $50 annual family membership fee include a discount telephone-buying service, two discount prescription-drug programs, associate membership in Club Costa Travel Club, an eye wear discount-purchase plan, and a legal protection plan. Members are also eligible to apply for insurance coverage under an NBA-sponsored plan.

Brennco Association Management provides management services for associations such as the National Benefit Association.

The Brennco Companies employ a total of 85 people.

Claims files are color-coded for quick and accurate reference. Brennco Benefit Administrators, the organization's flagship company, provides claims and other administrative services for approximately 30,000 insured persons. Photo by Jeff Locklear

DOUBLETREE HOTEL

The Doubletree Hotel at Corporate Woods is an executive meeting hotel located in Overland Park, one of the country's fastest-growing business and residential communities.

The hotel was the cornerstone of the Corporate Woods development that was built as a joint venture between Corporate Woods Associates, Jones & Company, and Metropolitan Life Insurance Company. Currently 21 office buildings, Bank IV, a shopping center, and the Doubletree comprise Corporate Woods. The Corporate Woods development, including the hotel, is a Metropolitan Life Insurance Company investment.

As the anchor of the business park's west end, the Doubletree answers a need for executive hotel space along Overland Park's flourishing College Boulevard. Begun in the mid-1970s, this five-mile corridor of glossy buildings and strong business development has experienced phenomenal growth. Forty-five of the *Fortune* 500 companies have a national, district, or regional presence on the boulevard. More than 80 insurance companies have major offices there as well.

In 1980 this growing corporate community cried out for restaurants and hotels. In 1982 the Doubletree opened to fill the need. Officially the second-largest hotel in Kansas, the Doubletree has 357 guest rooms, including 17 suites; 16,000 square feet of meeting space; and the 9,000-square-foot Grand Ballroom, which can accommodate 750 people for dinner. With its $10 million in total sales on about 70 percent annualized occupancy, the hotel exceeds the national average occupancy rate of about 60 percent.

The Doubletree offers 17 luxurious suites, some equipped with deluxe boardroom tables accommodating up to 10 people. They are a perfect setting for very private business conferences away from the bustle of the hotel's larger meeting rooms. Other suites feature tastefully appointed living areas to comfortably accommodate the "V.I.P." traveler. All take advantage of sweeping views of the Corporate Woods landscape through floor-to-ceiling windows. Photo by Steven Hicks

The Doubletree's inviting decor is a mix of modern and contemporary design with homey touches of country. Quilts, textured fabrics, and light-color woods give an air of openness and comfort.

Like a small, self-contained city, the hotel runs nonstop. A sophisticated computer-controlled fire- and life-safety system protects its guests around the clock.

Its 270 full- and part-time employees and the 30 managers who oversee the hotel's various operating departments are universally committed to giving each guest unsurpassed service. "Whether guests are here for a weekend vacation or an important

Each of the Doubletree's 357 guest rooms features a comfortable modern decor; a choice of queen, king, or two double beds; and cable television and in-room movies. Doubletree is famous for its special welcoming touch—homemade chocolate chip cookies delivered to each arriving guest's room. Photo by Steven Hicks

business meeting, the Doubletree's facilities meet every conceivable need," says Ric Tanner, the hotel's director of marketing.

The hotel has seven conference suites and a 50-seat audiovisual amphitheater, the only one of its kind in Kansas. This tiered learning center, with its permanent stage and lectern and sophisticated acoustics, provides a perfect setting for seminars.

The Overland Park Room, the second ballroom, has 1,300 square feet. A 4,000-square-foot prefunction gallery is perfect for receptions and exhibits.

The Butterfly Lounge, a popular spot with nightclub goers, soothes away stress as its dance music and disk jockey offer a pleasant contrast from day-long meetings.

No hotel is complete without a memorable restaurant, and the Doubletree offers the Rotisserie Restaurant and Grill. World-renowned chef George Lang developed the hotel's concept of a single restaurant with four distinct themes. The *Kansas City Star* newspaper gave the restaurant a four-star rating.

The Café, reminiscent of Europe's charming sidewalk cafés, is the perfect spot for morning coffee. The brisk and informal setting combined with good food make the Café just right for a quick pick-me-up throughout the day.

The Verandah recalls the midwestern gentility of bygone days. Under antebellum cloth canopies and rattan trellises, guests can savor genuine American cookery at its best.

The Kitchen combines excellent food service and a view of the preparation of a unique "appetite theatre buffet." There the restaurant's namesake rotisserie is center stage as chickens and ducks are roasted to perfection, surrounded by an extensive array of appetizers and salads.

The Parlour, set off from the rest of the restaurant by an actual indoor stream and waterfall, offers the best in fine dining. In understated elegance, guests savor the best prime rib Kansas City has to offer. Diners can enjoy classically simple or simply classic dining.

The Doubletree's kitchens prepare 330,000 meals per year—110,000 in the restaurants, 20,000 through room service, and 200,000 through catered affairs. The hotel has catered most of Kansas' state association meetings and has hosted the Johnson County Cancer Society Annual Gala. Each year this affair raises approximately $500,000, making it the second-largest U.S. fund-raising auction on behalf of the Cancer Society.

The Doubletree also has proved a perfect setting for weddings, reunions, and bar mitzvahs. Its courtyard and sun deck are delightful for receptions, cocktail parties, and barbecues.

The hotel plays an important part in the area's leisure and entertainment business. Located only 18 freeway minutes from downtown Kansas City, the Doubletree is convenient for sports enthusiasts and visitors to World's of Fun amusement park. The hotel bustles during baseball and football season, when fans come to town to cheer their favorite teams.

The Doubletree also is popular with folks yearning for a pampered weekend. Half of its weekend guests live in Johnson County, proving the Doubletree's neighbors know it is a perfect backyard retreat. Use of a nearby athletic club for tennis and golf, and the hotel's pool, spa, sauna, two racquetball courts, and jogging trails help guests escape from jobs, children, or the same old routine.

The Doubletree also offers affordable family plans and special rates to senior citizens through the American Association of Retired Persons. Because the business traveler accounts for almost one-third of the hotel's yearly business, the Doubletree offers special corporate programs and services to please its business clientele. The Gold Leaf program enables frequent business travelers and their reservation makers to redeem points for special services such as complimentary breakfasts, special rates, and mileage awards in conjunction with airlines.

Service remains the mainstay of Doubletree Inc., as well as the guiding philosophy in the firm's chain of 35 hotels in 16 states and 27 cities. To better measure its service performance, Doubletree Inc. created the

CARE index. At Doubletree hotels nationwide, guests are given scorecards and asked to rate the hotels. The score the hotel receives is posted at the front desk for everyone to see and becomes the "score to beat."

Eric Danziger, vice-president of Doubletree Inc., helped develop the CARE system. "We really do believe that the more we care, the more it shows," Danziger says, "and the more people will want to stay with us."

Superior service has given Doubletree Inc. a unique way to distinguish itself from the competition. Easy, friendly check-ins and check-outs and white-glove cleanliness are part of the hotel's superior service. So are bedtime snacks. Two freshly baked chocolate chip cookies greet guests at their bedside on their first-night's stay. These large, luscious cookies, each packing 440 calories, come from a secret recipe. Guests gobble up about 3 million per year. The chain now sells these popular cookies in specially designed tins.

STAR—Steps to Accent Recognition—preceded CARE. Doubletree's executives believe guests want to feel truly welcome and more than just another head in the bed. So in 1984 Doubletree began intensive employee education in genuine hospitality. STAR's guest recognition program includes three essentials: use of the guest's last name at all appropriate times, personal acknowledgement of returning guests, and a sincere and warm expression of thanks.

STAR continues to be a source of employee motivation and pride and an effective way of encouraging guests to return. The company's research shows CARE and STAR are working. Of those customers surveyed, 96 percent said they would return to a Doubletree hotel. The majority said the hotel's sincere and friendly personal service was the reason why.

In guest evaluation cards at the Doubletree Hotel at Corporate Woods, guests complimented the hotel and staff for a "generosity of spirit that pervades the hotel," and for its "service-oriented manner" and "smooth operation."

A dedication to service enabled G. Peter Bidstrup to transform Doubletree Inc. from one hotel in Scottsdale, Arizona, in 1969 to a national chain poised to become the leading name in upscale-lodging accommodations.

Bidstrup is the chairman of Doubletree Inc., and his hotel chain is now a subsidiary of Metropolitan Life Insurance Company, one of the nation's largest insurance and financial organizations. Total assets managed by Metropolitan Life and its affiliates exceed $100 billion, of which nearly $20 billion is invested in real estate.

Doubletree Hotel at Corporate Woods was one of the early joint ventures between Doubletree Inc. and Metropolitan Life and the one that brought the chain into Overland Park during the city's time of dynamic growth.

"We are happy to be part of the healthiest business environment in greater Kansas City," says John E. Green, general manager of the Doubletree at Corporate Woods. "Overland Park is one of the hottest suburban business centers in the United States and the best business marketplace in the state."

Mary Birch, executive vice-president and general manager of the Overland Park Chamber of Commerce, heartily agrees. "We've experienced a large amount of growth since our incorporation in 1960," Birch states. "Our strong financial health is unusual for a growing community. We have one of the state's lowest mill levies and are only a little over half-developed."

With more than 100,000 people, Overland Park is the fourth-largest city in Kansas and one of only 12 U.S. cities to have earned two AAA bond ratings. A local one-cent sales tax supports an aggressive capital improvement plan. Fifty-nine cents of every tax dollar paid goes into Overland Park's nationally recognized schools.

"Cooperation and compromise between an aggressive private sector, city government, and active chamber make Overland Park not only a successful business community, but also a nice place to live," Birch explains. "This spirit of cooperation and compromise helps us to get a lot done."

The Doubletree Hotel at Corporate Woods plays an active role in developing a strong business environment and community spirit. The hotel has sponsored the Peter Marshall Celebrity Golf Tournament and is the primary hotel sponsor for the Kansas Special Olympics. It contributes significantly to Overland Park's Chamber of Commerce and is an active member of the Overland Park Convention and Visitors Bureau, which got its start in 1983.

"The visitor industry has a strong economic impact on Overland Park," says Nick Jordan, the bureau's president. "When the bureau first started, visitors brought $110 million to the area. Today that figure is $270 million."

The Doubletree, Jordan believes, has played an important part in that growth, not only with its tourist business, but also with its conventions and business meetings.

Community leaders in Overland Park are working to establish a regional and local convention facility, a major dinner theater, and a significant educational and entertainment attraction. The Doubletree actively participates in those plans.

"Visitors to the Kansas City area appreciate having a safe and secure place to stay, with free parking and easy access to the city," Jordan says. "Overland Park has 14 hotel and motel facilities offering 2,500 rooms. The Doubletree is a great facility with reasonable rates. You can't find too many communities with such first-class choices."

One of the tallest buildings in Kansas, the Doubletree Hotel rises 18 stories over the beautiful Corporate Woods landscape. Photo by Steven Hicks

DOUBLETREE HOTEL

PATRONS

The following individuals, companies, and organizations have made a valuable commitment to the quality of this publication. Windsor Publications and the Kansas Department of Commerce gratefully acknowledge their participation in *Kansas: America, Center Stage.*

Barnes & Dodge, Inc.*
Bethany Medical Center*
Blue Cross and Blue Shield of Kansas*
The Brennco Companies*
Builders, Inc.*
Central Research Corporation*
Dillon Stores*
Fairbanks Morse Pump Corp.
Fleming Companies, Inc.*
Foulston & Siefkin*
Goodell, Stratton, Edmonds & Palmer*
Gossen Livingston Associates*
Greater Topeka Chamber of Commerce*
Hall-Kimbrell Environmental Service, Inc.*
High Plains Publishers, Inc.*
Hill's Pet Products, Division of Colgate Palmolive*
Kansas Association of Community Colleges*
Kansas College of Technology*
Kansas State University*
The Marley Company*
Reimer and Koger Associates, Inc.*
Ritchie Corporation*
St. Francis Hospital and Medical Center*
The Security Benefit Group of Companies*
Sheplers, Western Wear*
United Telecommunications, Inc.*
The University of Kansas*
Volume Shoe Corporation*
Wichita Area Chamber of Commerce*
Wichita Clinic P.A.*
The Wichita Eagle*
The Wichita State University*

*Participants in Part III, "Kansas' Enterprises." The stories of these companies and organizations appear in Chapters 9 through 13, beginning on page 123.

A field of sunflowers, after which the state was named, grow in a field near Atwood. Photo by Jeff Hetler. Courtesy, Unicorn Stock Photos

RESOURCES

PART I

Graves, Bill, office of. *Kansas Facts.* A publication of the Office of Secretary of State Bill Graves.

Gress, Tom. "Chains find the route to profit in Kansas slump." *Kansas City Business Journal,* May 11, 1987, pages 8-9.

Harper, Nan. "Lawrence, A Cultural Palette." *Horizon* magazine, September 1987, pages 24-25.

Maeroff, Gene I. "America's Top Public High Schools." *Town & Country* magazine, June 1986, page 146.

Mazerov, Katie. "The WSU/Pizza Hut Connection." *Wichita State Alumni Report,* July-August 1986, pages 10-15.

Perrin, Noel. "The old state fair, still what it used to be—even more." *Smithsonian* magazine, pages 97-108.

Prentis, Noel and Caroline. *History of Kansas.* Topeka: 1909.

Stratton, Joanna L. *Pioneer Women.* New York, N.Y.: Simon & Schuster, 1981.

Voigts, Madelyn. "Mission Hills." Mission Hills Homes Company.

Webster, Bayard. "The Menninger Clinic, A Farmhouse in 1925, Now A World Center." *New York Times,* November 13, 1975, pages 43, 69.

"USArts." *Horizon* magazine, September 1987, pages 19-22.

PART II

Bakers Way, February 1988, Vol. 11, No. 2.

Graves, Bill, office of. *Kansas Facts.* A publication of the Office of Secretary of State Bill Graves.

Kansas Board of Agriculture. *Kansas Farm Facts 1988.*

Kansas Business News, January 1988, Vol. 9, No. 1.

Kansas Cattle Feeding Industry Fact Sheet, June 1989.

Kansas Department of Commerce. "Kansas."

——. *Kansas International Trade Resource Directory.*

Kansas Department of Transportation. 1987 Selected Statistics.

——. 1988 Selected Statistics.

Kansas, Inc. Annual report, 1988.

——. "Business Plan '88."

Kansas Turnpike Authority. 36th annual report, 1988.

Kansas Wheat Commission. Annual report, 1988.

——. "Marketing Kansas Wheat."

"The Man Whose Lanterns Light Up the Countryside." *Nation's Business,* 1979.

Saab Aircraft Product Support. "Wing Tips," February 1988.

St. Louis Globe-Democrat, May 17, 1979.

"Sheldon Coleman, The Man Behind the Lantern." *Trailer Life* magazine, May 1986.

Wichita Airport Authority. Annual report, 1988.

——. *Mid-Continent Airport, 25th Anniversary, 1954-1979.*

Wichita Eagle, November 17, 1937, and November 20, 1937.

Yellow Freight System, Inc., of Delaware. Annual reports, 1983-1988.

INDEX

KANSAS' ENTERPRISES INDEX

GENERAL INDEX

Italicized numbers indicate illustrations.